$22.00

The Power of Feminist Theory

FEMINIST THEORY AND POLITICS

Alison Jaggar and Virginia Held, Series Editors

The Power of
Feminist Theory

Domination,
Resistance, Solidarity

Amy Allen

Westview Press
A Member of the Perseus Books Group

Feminist Theory and Politics

Copyright © 1999 by Westview Press, A Member of the Perseus Books Group

Published in 1999 in the United States of America by Westview Press, 5500 Central Avenue, Boulder, Colorado 80301-2877, and in the United Kingdom by Westview Press, 12 Hid's Copse Road, Cumnor Hill, Oxford OX2 9JJ

Library of Congress Cataloging-in-Publication Data
Allen, Amy.
    The power of feminist theory : domination, resistance, solidarity
/ by Amy Allen.
        p.   cm. — (Feminist theory and politics)
    Includes bibliographical references and index.
    ISBN 0-8133-9072-9
    1. Feminist theory.   2. Power (Social sciences).   I. Title.
II. Series.
HQ 1190.A434   1999
305.42'01—dc21   98-41071
                                                                        CIP

The paper used in this publication meets the requirements of the American National Standard for Permanence of Paper for Printed Library Materials Z39.48-1984.

10   9   8   7   6   5   4   3   2   1

for Clark

Contents

Acknowledgments

I have been very fortunate to have completed the early drafts of this project under the expert guidance of Nancy Fraser, whose vision and insight have helped me more than I can say. Thomas McCarthy and Jane Mansbridge also provided challenging yet sympathetic criticism throughout the process. James Bohman, Evelyn Brister, Susan Hekman, Richard Lynch, Kevin Olson, Vic Peterson, and Christopher Zurn read parts of the manuscript and offered many helpful comments. In addition, I have learned a great deal about feminism and about power from conversations with friends—in particular, Johanna Meehan, who nurtured this project and its author through the difficult stages of their development. Donna Chocol provided superb administrative support.

I am extremely grateful to Alison Jaggar for her enthusiastic support of this project and to Sarah Warner, Lisa Wigutoff, and Christine Arden of Westview Press for their patience and expertise.

Earlier versions of some chapters were presented at meetings of the Midwest Critical Theory Roundtable, the Society for Phenomenology and Existential Philosophy, and the Colloquium on Philosophy and the Social Sciences in Prague. I am grateful for the insights and criticisms of participants at those meetings.

My parents, Larry and Suzanne Allen, have always supported my intellectual pursuits, even when they did not care for them. For that, I am extremely grateful. My husband, Christopher Leazier, was not only a loving companion while I worked on this project but also read and commented on the manuscript and helped to compile the footnotes and bibliography. Although I certainly could have completed this project without him, I am infinitely grateful that I did not have to.

Earlier versions of some portions of this book have appeared in print before. A previous version of parts of Chapter 1 and Chapter 5 appeared as "Rethinking Power" in *Hypatia* 13, no. 1 (Winter 1998). Chapter 2 is a substantially revised version of "Foucault on Power: A Theory for Feminists," in Susan Hekman, ed., *Rereading the Canon: Feminist Interpretations of Foucault* (University Park: Pennsylvania State Press, 1997). I would like to thank Penn State Press for allowing me to reprint this material here. An earlier version of Chapter 3 appeared as "Power Trouble: Performativity as Critical Theory," in *Constellations* 5, no. 4 (December 1998). And portions of Chapter 4 appear in "Solidarity After Identity Politics: Hannah Arendt and the Power of Feminist Theory," in *Philosophy and Social Criticism* 25, no. 1 (January 1999).

Amy Allen

Introduction

Feminists have talked a great deal about power, so much so that it may seem as if nothing more remains to be said on the subject. This focus on power is not surprising, given the fact that, as Joan Scott has argued, "gender is a primary field within which or by means of which power is articulated."[1] If Scott is correct, then the feminist critique of gender necessitates a feminist critique of power. However, in what follows, I shall suggest that feminists have yet to develop a satisfactory account of this central concept. I have two primary tasks in this book: first, to assess contemporary feminist perspectives on power in an effort to explain why we have yet to come up with an adequate feminist conception of power; and second, to develop, by way of a consideration of the analyses of power offered by Michel Foucault, Judith Butler, and Hannah Arendt, a new feminist conception of power.

Edward Said has argued that, when thinking about power, "it is sensible to begin by asking the beginning questions, why imagine power in the first place, and what is the relationship between one's motive for imagining power and the image one ends up with."[2] Said goes on to suggest that the kind of conception of power one develops will depend in large part on the interest that one has in studying power in the first place, on what one wants a theory of power to do, on what kind of phenomena one wants this concept to illuminate.[3] Said's observation about the study of power helps us to make sense of how it is possible that completely disparate analyses can be put forth as accounts of one and the same concept. Thus, for instance, if we are interested primarily in thinking about the legitimate or illegitimate exercise of power by the state to constrain or limit the actions of the individual (as in classical liberal political theory), then we are likely to come up with a quite different conception than one whose thought about power is motivated by a concern with socioeconomic relations of oppression and stratification (as in, for example, classical Marxist political theory).

The observation that one's understanding of power is a function of the interests one brings to the study of power seems particularly true for feminist theorizing about power. After all, feminist theory is closely—although not uncritically—tied to the aims and interests of feminism as a social and political movement; thus, feminism clearly and unabashedly brings a particular set of interests to the table. If this is true, then it would make sense to ask ourselves at the outset "What interests feminists when we are interested in power?"[4] My initial answer to this question is the following: Insofar as feminists are interested in studying power, it is because we have an interest in understanding, criticizing, challenging, subverting, and ultimately overturning the multiple axes of stratification affecting women in contemporary Western societies, including (but not limited to) sexism, racism, heterosexism, and class oppression.[5]

If I am right in suggesting that this is the general motivation that feminist theorists bring to the analysis of power, then it follows that there are at least three specific interests that a feminist account of power must attempt to address. First, feminists have an interest in making visible and making sense of the systematic relations of sexist, racist, heterosexist, and class-based domination and subordination that characterize late capitalist Western pluralist societies. This concern requires an adequate feminist conception of power to shed light on power understood as domination. Indeed, it is this interest that motivates much of feminist research.

However, as both academic feminists and popular writers such as Katie Roiphe and Naomi Wolf have pointed out, a discussion of domination will not satisfy all of the interests that feminists have in studying power. By focusing too narrowly on domination, these critics maintain, feminists have obscured the power that women can exercise and have unwittingly portrayed women as victims.[6] Let me set aside for the moment the validity of these claims about feminist theory (I shall return to consider them in detail in Chapter 1) and note that they highlight a second interest that feminists have in studying power: specifically, the interest in thinking about the power that women are able to exercise even in spite of their subordination, a power that not only makes day-to-day living bearable and even pleasurable, but also makes resistance to domination possible. This interest requires a feminist conception of power to be able to adequately theorize empowerment and resistance.

However, given the incredibly complex and insidious forms that the subordination of women takes, it seems clear that the overturning of such subordination cannot be achieved simply through a bunch of individual acts of resistance. A collective feminist movement is also necessary; such a movement is made possible by the individual acts of resistance that go into putting it together and, in turn, provides conceptual and normative resources for individual women who are struggling to resist domination. Thus, feminists bring a third interest to the study of power, the interest in thinking about the collective power that binds the feminist movement together and allies it with related social movements. This interest requires a feminist conception to theorize power understood as solidarity.

The chief aim of this book is to develop a conception of power that meets these three requirements. I begin in Chapter 1 by critically assessing existing feminist conceptions of power. I examine three different conceptions of power that have been influential in feminist theory: power as resource, power as domination, and power as empowerment. I argue that, although each of these conceptions has provided important insights into women's experience, each is ultimately inadequate. The first is inadequate because it misconstrues the nature of power by understanding it as that which can be possessed, distributed, and redistributed, and the second and third are unsatisfactory because each of these conceptions emphasizes only one aspect of the multifaceted power relations that feminists are trying to understand. I argue that a better feminist conception would construe power as a relation rather than as a possession, but it would also avoid the tendency to mistake one aspect of power for the whole of it. Instead, it would highlight the complicated interplay between domination and empowerment.

In Chapter 2, I turn to Michel Foucault's highly original and provocative analysis of power for an account of power that begins to do just this. Given Foucault's emphasis on the interplay between constraint and enablement, feminists can find in Foucault resources for a conception of power that will illuminate the interplay between domination and empowerment or resistance. Thus, Foucault's account of power offers feminists a way of beginning to move beyond the problems associated with the accounts of power considered in Chapter 1. However, his account also has some crucial limitations. First, Foucault offers no way of making principled normative distinctions among problematic, neutral, and positive forms of constraint and/or enablement. Second, Foucault's account falls prey to a set of problems that I label the problem of resistance, the problem of agency, and the problem of solidarity.

In Chapter 3, I consider Judith Butler's feminist appropriation of Foucault's analysis of power as it is developed in her theory of the performativity of gender. I argue that, although Butler's earliest formulation of the theory of performativity in her book *Gender Trouble* falls prey to the same paradox of agency that plagues Foucault's analysis, her more recent reformulations enable her to move beyond this problem. For this reason, Butler's theory of gender performativity makes a significant contribution to a feminist critical theory of power. However, I maintain that there are several limitations to Butler's analysis that such a theory shall have to overcome. First, although Butler is perhaps more willing than Foucault to acknowledge that there might be a normative dimension to her analysis, she nevertheless fails to provide the kind of normative framework that is required by an analysis of power that purports to be critical—as a feminist analysis does. Second, unlike Foucault's account, Butler's suffers from too narrow a focus on the linguistic or discursive dimension of power and subjection. Although discourse is clearly a crucial medium for power relations, I argue that we cannot lose sight of the impact of the nondiscursive power relations on which Foucault's analysis focused. Finally, Butler's conception of power is unable to account for the collective power of feminist solidarity.

In contrast with Foucault's and Butler's accounts, Hannah Arendt's conception of power proves to be an excellent resource for thinking through the collective power of feminist solidarity. In fact, Arendt's analysis of power differs so starkly from Foucault's and Butler's that bringing these three theorists together might seem to be the height of theoretical poaching. However, I argue in Chapter 4 that the differences between Arendt and Foucault/Butler are not as stark as they might seem at first. In fact, these three share a number of philosophical commitments; and the philosophical differences between them, significant though they may be, do not pose insurmountable obstacles to an integration of their insights but instead serve as necessary correctives for the insufficiencies of the views of each. Having thus justified my placing of Arendt alongside Foucault and Butler, I go on to lay out Arendt's conception of power and argue that this conception offers a way of thinking about feminist solidarity that avoids the problematic essentialism that Butler and many other feminist critics are worried about.

In Chapter 5, I conclude by bringing together the elements of a feminist conception of power that emerge from my readings of Foucault, Butler, and Arendt. I draw on the best conceptual insights of each of these theorists: Foucault's analysis of the interplay between constraint and enablement, Butler's introduction of citationality as that which mediates between the constraint and the enablement of the subject, and Arendt's focus on the intersubjective emergence of power. I offer a definition of power that brings together the insights of these theorists but avoids the pitfalls of their conceptions of power as well. Furthermore, my conception is developed with an eye toward meeting the needs of a feminist critical theory of power. Thus, I arrive at my definition via a consideration of what it is that feminists are interested in when we are interested in power. In addition to offering a definition of power, I go on to offer some methodological prescriptions for studying power from a feminist perspective. I sketch out a series of analytic perspectives from which feminists ought to examine power relations. The result of these definitional and methodological considerations is a conception that enables us to theorize domination, resistance, and solidarity, and, perhaps more important, illuminates the interrelatedness of these three modalities of power. In other words, the result (I hope) is a conception of power that can meet the needs of feminist theory.

Notes

1. Joan Wallach Scott, *Gender and the Politics of History* (New York: Columbia University Press, 1988), p. 45.

2. Edward W. Said, "Foucault and the Imagination of Power," in David Couzens Hoy, ed., *Foucault: A Critical Reader* (Oxford: Blackwell, 1986), p. 151.

3. On this point, see also Steven Lukes, "Introduction," in Lukes, ed., *Power* (New York: New York University Press, 1986), p. 17.

4. This is a variation of the question posed by Lukes: "What interests us when we are interested in power?" See ibid., p. 17.

5. Of course, feminists also have a strong interest in understanding, criticizing, challenging, subverting, and ultimately overturning the domination relations that affect women around the world. However, if the interests that we have in the study of power are linked to the struggles of feminism as a social and political movement, and if these struggles vary in different cultures and societies because of the wide range of social, political, and cultural arrangements that exist, then it seems likely that the interests that Western feminists bring to the study of power will differ from those brought by non-Western feminists. But if we bring different interests to the study of power, then we are likely to come up with different ways of conceptualizing power. I mention this fact in order to emphasize that I am not attempting to develop a feminist conception of power that can apply universally; indeed, I suspect that it is impossible to develop such a conception. The conception of power that I develop in this book is thus somewhat limited in its scope; nevertheless, I hope that it will be useful for the complex and crucial task of theorizing the power relations that affect the lives of women in modern Western societies such as our own.

6. I discuss the scholarly debate on this issue in detail in Chapter 1. For the popular literature on so-called victim feminism, see Katie Roiphe, *The Morning After: Sex, Fear, and Feminism on Campus* (New York: Little, Brown, 1993); and Naomi Wolf, *Fire with Fire: The New Female Power and How It Will Change the 21st Century* (New York: Random House, 1993).

1

Feminist Conceptions of Power: A Critical Assessment

Power is clearly a crucial concept for feminist theory. Whatever else feminists may be interested in, we are certainly interested in understanding the way that gender, race, class, and sexuality intersect with power. However, assessing feminist conceptions of power is not an easy task, since these conceptions tend to be implicit in feminist writings, rather than explicitly discussed and defended. Thus, the first task involved in assessing these conceptions is to reconstruct the conceptions of power that have been presupposed by feminist theorists. In this chapter, I reconstruct three ways of conceptualizing power that have been implicit (and sometimes explicit) in various approaches to feminist theory. The first conception understands power as a positive social good, a resource, the distribution of which among men and women is currently unequal. It thus sees the goal of feminism to be a redistribution of this positive resource so that women will have power in amounts roughly equal to men. The second understands power not as a resource that can be possessed, distributed, or redistributed but, rather, as a relation—specifically, a relation of (male) domination and (female) subordination. This view equates power with domination and domination with a set of pervasive, dyadic, master/subject relations through which gender is created and reinforced. From this perspective, the goal of feminism is not to enable women to have power in amounts roughly equal to men but to dismantle the system of domination entirely. The third view rejects each of these understandings in favor of a positive conception of power as empowerment or transformation. According to this view, power is a positive capacity that grows out of feminine traits, capacities, or practices; conceptualized in this way, women's power becomes the basis for a wholesale revision of the masculinist conceptions of social and political life that have been at the fore of Western political thought.

In the present chapter, I examine in more detail each of these feminist conceptions of power. Along the way, I also consider the criticisms of each view that have been raised by feminists. I shall argue that, although feminists have been right to reject the distributive model of power as resource, we have yet to develop an alternate conception that can do justice to the complex and multifarious power relations that feminism seeks to critique and to transform. Specifically, I shall argue that the conceptions of power as domination and power as empowerment reify power as a whole into only one of its aspects, and that, as a result, each of these conceptions offers a distorted picture of women's situation. My point here is that these conceptions of power are not so much wrong as they are incomplete. A better feminist conception would be one that resisted the impulse to collapse power into either domination or empowerment but, instead, highlighted the complicated interplay between these two modalities of power.

Power as Resource

The conception of power as a resource that women ought to have in amounts equal to men has been perhaps the most influential conception throughout the history of the feminist movement. Something like this conception of power is presupposed in John Stuart Mill's *The Subjection of Women*[1] and in many of the other liberal feminist perspectives developed since Mill. The main argument of *The Subjection of Women* is that the promise of liberal political philosophy, including equal opportunity with respect to the most fundamental form of exercise of political power—namely, voting—ought to be extended to women. In Mill's view, political power is a resource that most, if not all, men have and most, if not all, women do not; Mill's feminism calls for granting women access to this resource through, among other things, an extension of the franchise to women. The problem that feminism aims to solve, in this view, is that women are excluded from or not represented within the political sphere; the solution is adequate representation and inclusion in this sphere. In other words, the problem with respect to power is a problem of distribution among men and women; the solution is equality of opportunity with respect to political power; the goal is to get to a point where women have such power alongside men.

In the twentieth century, this conception of power has been expanded and elaborated upon by Susan Moller Okin. In *Justice, Gender, and the Family*,[2] Okin argues persuasively that we must extend the principles of justice and apply them to the "private" sphere of the family. By making this argument, Okin expands considerably on what Mill (along with the majority of Western political philosophers) takes to be the proper scope of the political domain.³ Nevertheless, Okin seems to retain Mill's conception of power as a resource that is currently denied to women, while at the same time extending this conception to encompass not only the relationship of women to the state but also their relationships to husbands in traditional gender-structured families and the implications of these familial relationships for women's relative powerlessness vis-à-vis the state and the workplace. Thus, Okin's goal is similar to Mill's—she calls for a redistribution of power such that women will have equal access to this valuable resource in the related domains of family, workplace, and public sphere—even though her account of what it would take to achieve this goal is very different from his.

Okin's main argument is that the contemporary gender-structured family is unjust in that the benefits and burdens of familial life are distributed among men (husbands/fathers) and women (wives/mothers) in systematically unequal ways. Power, according to Okin, is one of the benefits that is maldistributed in such families. As she puts it, "When we look seriously at the distribution between husbands and wives of such critical social goods as work (paid and unpaid), power, prestige, self-esteem, opportunities for self-development, and both physical and economic security, we find socially constructed inequalities between them, right down the list."⁴ Here, power is cast explicitly as a "critical social good," as an important resource; the implication is that it is *prima facie* unjust to give power to some people while denying it to others. According to Okin, the unequal distribution of power and other resources within the family is the result of a variety of institutional and structural social factors, but the linchpin of all of these is the gender division of paid and unpaid labor and the corresponding cultural system of valuation that deems paid "productive" labor valuable and unpaid "reproductive" labor valueless. This set of social and cultural forces renders women vulnerable in systematic ways. As Okin sums up her argument:

> Women are made vulnerable by constructing their lives around the expectation that they will be primary parents; they become more vulnerable within marriages in which they fulfill this expectation, whether or not they also work for wages; and they are most vulnerable in the event of separation or divorce, when they usually take over responsibility for children without adequate support from their ex-husbands.⁵

Given that her critique of current power relations rests on the presumption that power is a positive social resource, equal access to which is largely denied to women, Okin's goal is to redistribute power by redistributing labor in the family: "We must work toward eradicating the socially created vulnerabilities of women that stem from the division of la-

bor and the resultant division of power within it."[6] In other words, the
goal is an equal sharing of paid and unpaid labor that, in turn, will redistribute power and other critical social goods equally. Thus, as with Mill,
Okin presumes that power is a positive resource, a good; further, she presupposes that, with respect to power, the problem that feminists should
be concerned with is one of distribution. In short, Okin's account rests on
the belief that the goal of feminism is to get to a point where women *have*
power in amounts roughly equal to men.

Iris Marion Young has offered an insightful critique of the kind of distributive model of power presupposed by both Mill and Okin. As Young
describes this model, "Conceptualizing power in distributive terms
means implicitly or explicitly conceiving power as a kind of stuff possessed by individual agents in greater or lesser amounts. From this perspective a power structure or power relations will be described as a pattern of the distribution of this stuff."[7] Young points out four problems
with this way of conceiving of power. First, this model obscures the fact
that "power is a relation rather than a thing."[8] Although the ability to exercise power may be enhanced by the possession of certain key resources
(money, self-esteem, weapons, education, political influence, physical
strength, social authority, and so on), this ability should not be conflated
with those resources themselves. Second, the distributive model tends toward a dyadic understanding of power: "a focus on particular agents or
roles that have power, and on agents over whom these powerful agents
or roles have power."[9] In other words, this conception tends to encourage
thinking of a master/subject relationship as the paradigmatic power relation. The problem with a dyadic conception is that it "misses the larger
structure of agents and actions that mediates between two agents in a
power relation."[10] Third, the distributive conception of power incorrectly
views power relations as static patterns rather than as dynamic
processes. According to Young, "A distributive understanding of power
obscures the fact that, as Foucault puts it, power exists only in action."[11]
Finally, this conception of power misunderstands the nature of domination; it "conceive[s] of a system of domination as one in which power,
like wealth, is concentrated in the hands of the few. . . . A redistribution of
power is called for, which will disperse and decentralize power so that a
few individuals or groups no longer have all or most of the power."[12] If
power is conceived of in this way, the following problem arises: Given
that those who are subordinated don't currently have power, then how
are they to wield the power that is needed to change social relationships
such that they will be granted equal access to this critical resource? It
seems clear that, as far as the power-as-resource model goes, subordinate
groups are simply incapable of wielding such power. Not only does this
seem a dubious claim in and of itself, but the acceptance of this claim also

leaves Mill and Okin in the uncomfortable position of depending upon the state to grant women equal access to power. Thus, the conception of power as an unequally distributed resource seems to rely implicitly on what Anna Yeatman has described as a

> state centric form of "power over" which reconstitutes the standing of those who are to be protected as subjects in need of protection, and as subjects who are likely to be victimized without this protection. When women are in- cluded within the category of such subjects, this particular type of "femi- nization" of women functions to inscribe them discursively as subjects who depend on the protective power of the state.[13]

For all of these reasons, the feminist conception of power as a *resource* that women ought to *have* in amounts roughly equal to men is inade- quate.

Power as Domination

A second conception of power can be reconstructed from the work of so- called radical feminists such as Catharine MacKinnon, Andrea Dworkin, and Carole Pateman; instead of viewing power as a positive social re- source that women ought to possess in amounts equal to men, these fem- inists tend to describe power as a relation of domination and subordina- tion. Thus, their goal is not a redistribution of power but a dismantling of the system of male domination and female subordination altogether.

The view of power presupposed by these feminists is closely related to their understanding of gender difference. MacKinnon, Dworkin, and Pateman each reject a view that claims or assumes that gender differ- ences are natural or innate and that whatever imbalances of power that exist are laid over these natural differences. This kind of understanding of gender incorrectly assumes that differences between men and women are not in themselves problematic; instead, what are problematic are the costs and benefits unjustly attached to these differences. The goal for those who accept this understanding of gender then becomes taking away the costs of differences and restoring differences to their unprob- lematic state. MacKinnon sums up this conventional view of gender as follows: "On the first day, difference was; on the second day, a division was erected upon it; on the third day, irrational instances of domination arose. Division may be rational or irrational. Dominance either is or seems justified. Difference *is*."[14]

In contrast with this conventional view of gender, MacKinnon, Dworkin, and Pateman explain differences between men and women as a function of domination: In their view, relations of domination are prior to differences between men and women, and the emphasis on difference is introduced after the fact for the purpose of justifying and maintaining that system of dominance. Differences between men and women, then, are simply the reified effects of dominance.[15] As MacKinnon puts the point, "Difference is the velvet glove on the iron fist of domination. The problem is not that differences are not valued; the problem is that they are defined by power."[16] MacKinnon makes it clear that, in her view, power is equated with domination, and that domination and gender are completely interrelated, such that relations of domination are implicated in the very formation of gender difference itself. When you think about it this way, it is no wonder that there are significant differences between men and women; as MacKinnon puts it: "I mean, can you imagine elevating one half of a population and denigrating the other half and producing a population in which everyone is the same?"[17] Thus, according to this conception of power, it makes no sense to think of power as a stuff that men possess more of than women; instead, power is responsible for the very formation of "men" and "women." In other words, as MacKinnon puts it, "men are the way they are because they have power, more than that they have power because they are the way they are. If this is so, women who succeed to male forms of power will largely be that way too."[18] Thus, it seems clear that the goal for domination theorists is not to grant women equal access to power but, instead, to dismantle the very system of domination itself.

The upshot of this view of gender difference as a domination relation is that women are powerless and men are powerful as such. This is evinced by MacKinnon's claim that "women/men is a distinction not just of difference, but of power and powerlessness. . . . Power/powerlessness *is* the sex difference."[19] Carole Pateman puts the point somewhat differently, but the upshot is the same: "The patriarchal construction of the difference between masculinity and femininity is the political difference between freedom and subjection."[20] In other words, to be masculine, to have the characteristics that our culture attributes to males, is to be free, whereas to be feminine is to be subjected. According to this view of power as domination, what it means to be a woman is to be powerless, and what it means to be a man is to be powerful.

If men are powerful and women powerless as such, then the domination relation between men and women will, of necessity, be pervasive; that is to say, it will exist wherever there are people who are socially defined (i.e., gendered) as men or women. This means that all men are in a position of dominance over women, and, as a corollary to this view, that all women are in a subordinate position vis-à-vis men. This does not mean that all men wield the *same kind* of power over all women; theorists who accept this view are quick to recognize that, for example, men of color do not generally wield the same sort of power over white women that many white men have been able to exercise. Nevertheless, these theorists maintain that they are in some sense in a position of dominance with respect to white women; thus, the claim that all men are in a position of power over women is, on their view, justified.

Pateman, for example, expressly claims that all men are in a position of dominance over women simply because they are men: "In modern civil society all men are deemed good enough to be women's masters."[21] Her contention that all men are deemed good enough to be women's masters might seem to imply the weak claim that all men are *capable* of exercising power over women, as opposed to the strong claim that they do in fact exercise such power. According to Pateman, however, it does not: "The power is still there even if, in any individual case, it is not used."[22] That is to say, men's power consists in their ability to exercise power over women at any time and for any reason; even the most benevolent of men can avail himself of this power if he so chooses. According to Pateman, this is "the form of political right that all men exercise by virtue of being men."[23] Moreover, Pateman indicates that she accepts the corollary to this claim—namely, that all women are in a subordinate position with respect to men. As I pointed out above, Pateman equates femininity with subjection, which implies that all women, insofar as they are feminine, are subject to male masters. As a result, on Pateman's analysis, male domination appears to be pervasive.

MacKinnon likewise accepts the claim that all men are in a position of power over women. She maintains that it is a basic "fact of male supremacy" that "no woman escapes the meaning of being a woman within a gendered social system, and sex inequality is not only pervasive but may be universal (in the sense of never having not been in some form)."[24] If the meaning of being a woman is being powerless (subordinate), just as the meaning of being a man is being powerful (dominant), and if no woman (or man) within a gendered social system escapes this, then all men are powerful and all women are powerless.

Like MacKinnon and Pateman, Dworkin contends that male domination is pervasive. Dworkin, however, emphasizes the fact that this relation is far from identical in all instances. She acknowledges that certain men cannot wield certain kinds of power over certain women due to their race, ethnic background, or class. Nevertheless, this fact does not change the general point in Dworkin's eyes. As she puts it,

> Intercourse occurs in a context of a power relation that is *pervasive and incontrovertible*. The context in which the act takes place . . . is one in which men have social, economic, political, and physical power over women. Some men do not have all these kinds of power over all women; *but all men have*

some kinds of power over all women; and most men have controlling power over what they call their women—the women they fuck.[25]

In Dworkin's view, as on this view of power as domination in general, all men exercise some kind of power—be it social, economic, political, or physical—over all women, and all women are subject to men in some way or another.

In addition to claiming that power is a relation of male dominance and female subordination, and that this relation is pervasive, these theorists often assume a particular understanding of how domination functions. In their view, domination tends to be understood dyadically, on the model of a master/subject relation. Nancy Fraser has described this account of domination, which she criticizes Pateman for adopting, as follows: "Women's subordination is understood first and foremost as the condition of being subject to the direct command of an individual man."[26] Indeed, Pateman's reliance on the master/subject understanding of domination is evident in her claim that "to understand modern patriarchy, . . . it is necessary to keep the contract between master and servant or master and slave firmly in mind."[27] Pateman's version of this view of power as a dyadic domination relation emerges out of her critique of classical social contract theory. According to her analysis, the original contract said to initiate civil society is both social and sexual. It is social in the sense that it provides for the possibility of the legitimate exercise of political rights. Further, "it is sexual in the sense of patriarchal—that is, the contract establishes men's political right over women—and also sexual in the sense of establishing orderly access by men to women's bodies."[28] In other words, the social/sexual contract establishes a series of social relations whereby individual men are put in a position of dominance over individual women; it thus creates what Pateman calls the "law of male sex-right," which men exercise by sexually subjugating women—that is, by becoming their sexual masters.[29] As Fraser puts the point, "The sexual contract . . . establishes and democratizes 'male sex-right,' the right of individual men to command individual women—in labor and especially in sex. It institutes a series of male/female master/subject dyads."[30]

MacKinnon and Dworkin likewise presuppose this view of domination as a dyadic, master/subject relation. For them, however, it is not derived from a critique of classical contractarianism; rather, it is a logical consequence of their claim that sexual intercourse is the paradigm case of men's domination over women. As MacKinnon puts it, "the social relation between the sexes is organized so that men may dominate and women must submit and this relation is sexual—in fact, is sex."[31] Similarly, Dworkin claims that the [sexual] act itself, without more, is the possession. There need not be a social relationship in which the woman is subordinate to the man. . . . There need not be an ongoing sexual relationship in which she is chronically, demonstrably, submissive or masochistic. The normal fuck by a normal man is taken to be an act of invasion and ownership undertaken in a mode of predation: colonializing, forceful (manly) or nearly violent; the sexual act that *by its nature* makes her his.[32]

According to MacKinnon and Dworkin, the violence and exploitation inherent in the very nature of heterosexual intercourse in our culture provide the model for other instances of male supremacy, such as pornography, battery, rape, and sexual harassment. In MacKinnon and Dworkin's view, then, heterosexual intercourse, which generally takes place between an individual man and an individual woman, is the paradigm case of male domination. Insofar as their account of domination is modeled on a dyadic relation, the account itself is best understood as dyadic—that is, as illuminating the relationship between sexual masters and their subjects. Indeed, that they presuppose this dyadic account of domination is evidenced by one of the more memorable images employed by both Dworkin and MacKinnon, the image that compares male power to a foot placed firmly on women's necks. Consider Dworkin's description of the goal she envisions for feminism: "I want real change, an end to the social power of men over women; more starkly, his boot off my neck."[33] As loaded as it may seem, this image is actually quite appropriate given MacKinnon and Dworkin's understanding of power; each of these theorists seems to presuppose that power is the domination that individual men wield over individual women, aptly exemplified by the image of the male master standing triumphantly over his prone female subject, his boot on her neck, holding her in place.

Fraser has provided an insightful critique of this kind of characterization of male dominance as a dyadic, master/subject relation. She contends that such a characterization provides an inaccurate picture of women's subordination in contemporary Western industrialized societies. Specifically, she writes, "gender inequality is today being transformed by a shift from dyadic relations of mastery and subjection to more impersonal structural mechanisms that are lived through more fluid cultural forms."[34] In other words, conceiving of domination on a dyadic model is insufficiently structural; such a conception simply fails to make sense of the complex structural mechanisms at work in contemporary Western societies that both reinforce and provide the opportunity for subverting women's subordination.

The equation of power with domination and of domination with a master/subject model not only distorts the nature of gender inequality, it also distorts the ways that inequalities of race, class, and sexuality are intertwined with those of gender. Elizabeth Spelman makes this point with respect to the claim that all men exercise power over women. To say this, according to Spelman,

> makes it look as if my relationship to the bank vice president I am asking for a loan is just like my relationship to the man who empties my wastebasket at the office each night; similarly, it makes it look as if their relationship to me is no different from their relationship to the woman who cleans the halls of the administration building.[35]

Spelman's worry is that the blanket claim that all men are in a position of power over all women obscures the racism, class oppression (and, we might add, heterosexism) that are interwoven with and integral to the subordination of women. To say that all men are in a position of dominance over all women is, in her view, to ignore the difference that difference makes with respect to such dominance.

As I pointed out above, those who presuppose this conception of power as domination do not argue that all men wield the same kind of power over all women; that is to say, they acknowledge that racial, ethnic, and class differences help to determine what kind of power particular men will be able to wield over particular women. Nevertheless, Spelman's point is on target: Simply saying that different men have access to different kinds of power is a far cry from attempting to understand and illuminate the nature of those differences. Saying that all men dominate women and that all women are dominated by men implies that it is possible to talk unproblematically about "women as women," a stance that, as Spelman points out, "has the effect of making certain women rather than others paradigmatic examples of 'women'—namely, those women who seem to have a gender identity untainted (I use the word advisedly) by racial or class identity."[36] By claiming that the domination relation is one that holds between men and women as such, domination theorists render themselves unable to fully illuminate relations of power grounded in race, class, ethnicity, and sexuality that obtain among women (and among men), and that have a profound impact on the intersection of power and gender.

A further problem with this view of power emerges when one considers the question of resistance. Despite, or perhaps as a result of, their rather pessimistic picture of the domination relations that obtain between men and women, these theorists still endeavor to give some account of the capacity that women have to resist male power. Indeed, their writings make no sense unless one assumes that the point of their discussing male domination in the first place is to inspire women to fight back; they seem to believe that if they get women angry enough about our situation, we will go out and start resisting. However, by claiming that women are powerless and men powerful as such, domination theorists have denied themselves the theoretical resources necessary for an adequate conceptualization of women's resistance to oppression. Just as the power-as-resource model is ultimately unable to conceptualize how women might use power in their struggle against male dominance, the power-as-domination model renders invisible all instances in which women assert their own power over and against forces of domination. With this in mind, it is not surprising that MacKinnon claims that female power is "a contradiction in terms, socially speaking."[37] Having claimed that power is by definition male, MacKinnon—and those who understand power in this way—cannot help but view female power as a contradiction in terms.

Nevertheless, these theorists continue to talk about women's resistance to male domination. For example, Pateman claims that our understanding of the social/sexual contract "is only possible because women (and some men) have resisted and criticized patriarchal relations since the seventeenth century."[38] Similarly, MacKinnon enjoins her readers to "take the unknowable more seriously than anyone ever has, because most women have died without a trace; but *invent the capacity to act*, because otherwise women will continue to."[39] Ultimately, all that this conception of power can tell us about the power that women do have, about our capacity to act, is that, in the face of pervasive and incontrovertible domination, we must invent that capacity. Unfortunately, however, as a result of its one-sided emphasis on power as domination, this conception of power cannot offer us the theoretical resources that might help us envision such an invention.

In addition to making it impossible to understand women's resistance to male domination, this conception of power leads to the final problem of ushering in what Yeatman calls a politics of *ressentiment*:

> When a movement understands itself as representing those who are powerless, the victims of the powerful, it neither permits itself responsibility for, nor engagement in the affairs of the world. It maintains an innocence of worldly affairs, and in particular an innocence in regard to power. It does not confront the truths that power inheres in all relationships, that any interpretation of reality is itself a manifestation of power, and that those who are relatively powerless still participate in power.[40]

In other words, this conception of power not only denies the power that some women wield over others on the basis of their racial, ethnic, class, or heterosexual privilege, it also denies the power that women wield when we engage in political struggle for feminist causes, and even when we offer a feminist theoretical interpretation of the world. Ironically, although MacKinnon, Dworkin, and Pateman offer compelling feminist interpretations of political realities, the conception of power that they presuppose makes it difficult for them to account for their own power to develop such interpretations.

To its credit, the conception of power as a relation of male domination and female subordination avoids some of the limitations of the power-as-resource model. Instead of thinking of power primarily as a kind of stuff that men have and women don't, the power-as-domination model sees power as something that exists only in relation. However, this model still conceives of power as a static, dyadic, master/subject relation. As a result, this conception of power has a hard time explaining how someone could be subordinate in one respect (by virtue of being a woman) and yet be dominant in another respect (by virtue of being a white, upper-middle-class, heterosexual woman). And it has a hard time explaining how those who are socially defined as powerless will ever be able to wield the kind of power necessary for changing society. Both of these difficulties stem from the fact that this conception of power overemphasizes domination and, thus, ignores the dynamic interplay between domination and empowerment, between power and counterpower.

Power as Empowerment

A third feminist conception of power emerged in part as a response to the shortcomings of the conceptions of power as resource and power as domination—in particular, the difficulty these conceptions have of accounting for the power that women are able to exercise, what we might call the power of the powerless. Feminists who conceptualize power as empowerment do of course acknowledge that, in patriarchal societies, men are in a position of dominance over women; but they choose to focus on a different understanding of power: power as the ability to empower and transform oneself, others, and the world. This conception of power as empowerment is based on the contention that women have special skills and traits that have been devalued by misogynist cultures; in particular, women are said to place a greater emphasis on care and on the maintenance of relationships with other adults, with children, and with the earth itself. Feminists who embrace this conception then go on to argue that this "care perspective" provides the basis for a beneficial, even revolutionary, understanding of power as empowerment that ought to be the basis for a feminist revisioning of society.

The notion that women place a greater emphasis than men on preserving relationships was given its definitive presentation by Carol Gilligan. Gilligan's research uncovered a putative difference in the moral development of highly educated men and women in the United States: Whereas the men tended to be more concerned with autonomy, individuation, and justice, some of the women tended to be more oriented toward responsibility to and concern for others.[41] As Gilligan notes, "The psychology of women . . . has consistently been described as distinctive in its greater orientation toward relationships and interdependence."[42] Due to this emphasis on care, women were traditionally thought to lag behind men in terms of moral development. By contrast, Gilligan and other, more recent empowerment theorists seek to reinterpret women's care perspective as a distinctive strength.

Whereas Gilligan elaborates the care perspective with respect to relationships in general, some empowerment theorists have zeroed in on the mother-child relationship as the most important for understanding women's supposedly unique perspective on social life. Building on the work of Gilligan and others, Sara Ruddick and Virginia Held both see the practice of mothering as central to a feminist revisioning of society. According to Ruddick and Held, the practice of mothering requires mothers to preserve, nurture, and empower their children. The preserving, nurturing, and empowering abilities that mothers have developed are then taken as the basis for a new feminist understanding of social interaction. To be sure, both Ruddick and Held acknowledge the fact that men can be mothers: Mothering is a social practice, not a natural ability, and a mother is simply one who has primary responsibility for nurturing and caring for children and, thus, is not necessarily a woman.[43] However, since most mothers have been and continue to be women, and since maternal thinking arises out of motherhood as a practice, most maternal thinkers are women. Accordingly, these empowerment theorists are describing a perspective that is, for the most part, still specific to women.

For our purposes, the important claim made by empowerment theorists is not just that these maternal and care perspectives are more or less unique to women, but that they provide the basis for a new way to think about power. As Jean Baker Miller puts the point, "women's examination of power . . . can bring new understanding to the whole concept of power."[44] This reexamination of power from women's perspective is also evident in the work of Gilligan. Gilligan believes that when women reach the highest stage of moral development where such development is understood in terms of care (rather than autonomy)—that is, the stage where they learn to integrate care for themselves with care for others—they thereby experience a sense of empowerment. Thus, she claims that one of her subjects who had attained this stage had thereby gained "an acknowledgment of her own power and worth."[45] She describes another stage-three subject in a similar way: "No longer feeling so powerless, exploited, alone, and endangered, Betty feels more in control."[46]

Held, by contrast, views the specific experiences of women who are mothers as the source for a reexamination of the concept of power. She writes that "the capacity to give birth and to nurture and empower could be the basis for new and more humanly promising conceptions than the ones that now prevail of power, empowerment, and growth."[47] This new understanding will replace the old masculinist conception, according to which power is "the power to cause others to submit to one's will, the power that led men to seek hierarchical control and . . . contractual restraints."[48] In other words, in Held's view, the old, unpromising, male conception of power and control as domination—precisely the conception presupposed in the power-as-domination view discussed above— ought to be replaced by a conception that draws on the experience of nurturance and empowerment that women gain through being mothers.

Reference to women's unique and empowering experience of power can also be found in feminist works that emphasize lesbian and women's spirituality. For instance, in her discussion of women's spirituality, Starhawk claims: "I am on the side of the power that emerges from within, that is inherent in us as the power to grow is inherent in the seed."[49] According to Starhawk, this power-from-within is the life-affirming and sustaining force at the heart of lesbian and women's spirituality. Once again, this understanding of a positive, empowering use of power is contrasted with the masculine conception of power, which, as Sarah Hoagland puts it, "focus[es] on state authority, police and armed forces, control of economic resources, control of technology, and hierarchy and chain of command."[50] The point of feminist investigations into power, according to this view, is to challenge the presupposition that power equals control or domination, and to replace this view with a conception that is based on women's more positive, life-affirming experience of empowerment or power-from-within.[51]

However, the question remains: What kind of conception does women's positive, life-affirming experience with power lead us to adopt? Miller's definition of the power that women experience is "the capacity to produce a change."[52] Similarly, Ruddick claims that to have power as mothers experience it is "to have the individual strength or the collective resources to pursue one's pleasures and projects."[53] Hoagland echoes this point: "'Power-from-within' is the power of ability, of choice and engagement. It is creative; and hence it is an affecting and transforming power, but not a controlling power."[54] Hélène Cixous makes a similar claim— namely, that "les pouvoirs de la femme" are not a question of power over others but "a question of power over oneself, in other words of a relation not of mastery but of availability."[55] Thus, Cixous suggests that women's experience of power is not one of domination or control but of ability, capacity, and individual empowerment. In other words, according to this conception, power is a capacity or creative ability that individuals have *to do* something, rather than a dominance that is wielded *over* others. First and foremost, then, the conception of power derived from women's experience is a positive one: Instead of equating power with domination or control, this conception sees power as the capacity or ability to pursue certain life projects.

Many of these theorists make the further claim that women's experience of power has the characteristic of fostering or nurturing the ability or capacity of others to pursue their own life projects. As Held puts the point: "The power of a mothering person to empower others, to foster transformative growth, is a different sort of power from that of a stronger sword or a dominant will."[56] In Held's view, power is not just any capacity: It is the capacity to transform and empower oneself and others. Miller makes a similar point: "There is enormous validity in women's not wanting to use power as it is presently conceived and used. Rather, women may want to be powerful in ways that simultaneously enhance, rather than diminish, the power of others."[57] This conception of power as transformative and empowering is echoed in the work of Luce Irigaray. Irigaray maintains that part of the task of feminism must be to question the way that power itself has been understood in phallocentric cultures, for if feminists "aim simply for a change in the distribution of power, leaving intact the power structure itself, then they are resubjecting themselves, deliberately or not, to a phallocratic order."[58] In order to break free of the phallocratic order, we have to avoid explaining women's situation with reference to "a definition of power of the masculine type."[59] Instead, Irigaray envisions a transformative power that is grounded in a feminine economy—an economy whose paradigm is the mother-daughter relationship.[60]

Indeed, insofar as women may use their power to empower others, the ultimate goal of this particular use of power is to render itself superfluous.[61] According to this view, power is the ability to transform and empower others by nurturing and caring for them in such a way that they are ultimately able to be powerful themselves. As Thomas Wartenberg shows, feminists who accept this conception see mothers' power as transformative in that it transforms the child into a powerful being who is no longer subject to maternal power; in other words, maternal, feminine power is, as Wartenberg puts it, "self-transcending."[62]

Wartenberg has raised a potential problem with feminists' account of what he calls "the transformative use of power."[63] In his view, feminists who have seen the power of mothers as empowering and transformative have based this conception on the following claim: "[A]lthough women are not socially dominant—they lack power-over—they do have special skills and abilities that have been ignored or devalued by traditional valuations but that enable them to act in important and valuable ways—they have power-to."[64] However, Wartenberg contends that these feminists have an inadequate and misleading way of understanding their own conception of power. He argues that the kind of power that women experience as mothers does "involve the *power* that women have *over* other social agents [for example, children]; however, it is a use of power-over for a purpose other than social *domination*."[65] In other words, Wartenberg claims that proponents of the power-as-empowerment view misunderstand the nature of mothers' power when they claim that it is a fundamentally different sort of power than domination. On the contrary, he contends that *both* women's transformative power *and* men's dominating power are instances of exercising power over others; the only difference between the two is that the former is a benevolent and the latter a malevolent use of such power.

Wartenberg is correct in pointing out that mothers' transformative and empowering use of power often involves the exercise of power over others, and he is right in emphasizing that this power need not be considered an instance of domination, insofar as it may be exercised for the benefit of the subordinate agent. However, it seems to me that the strict distinction between power-over and power-to on which his critique relies cannot be maintained. Although I agree that these two ways of exercising power can be distinguished analytically (and I offer my own way of distinguishing them in Chapter 5), I think it is too strong to say, as Wartenberg does, that "the phrases 'has power to' and 'has power over' are not, despite their lexical similarity, about the same concept—'power.'"[66] Wartenberg maintains that the fundamental difference between power-over and power-to is that the former is necessarily relational whereas the latter is not.[67] In other words, according to Wartenberg, one can make sense of the concept of power-over only by thinking of a social relation in which one agent has or exercises power over another, but one need not think of a social relation in order to make sense of the concept of power-to (which he understands as "simply an ability"[68]). But this latter claim seems false. Certain biological capacities and abilities (breathing, digestion, and the like) aside, how else do human beings acquire our abilities and capacities to do things, if not through our social relationships with others? Given that this is the case, it seems clear that social relations are the condition of possibility for the capacities and abilities (the power-to) of the individual. Moreover, as I shall argue in Chapters 2 and 3, if social relations between men and women in societies such as ours are structured by domination, and if men and women come to have the capacities and abilities that they have as a result of their social relations with others, then one of the most important issues for feminist theorists of power to grapple with is how to understand the complex interplay between power-over and power-to. But if

power-to is no less relational than power-over, and if the distinction between these two uses of power is not as sharp as Wartenberg maintains,
then his attempt to reduce transformative power to an instance of power-
over is problematic.

Thus, it seems too strong to contend, as Wartenberg does, that those
who accept the power-as-empowerment view misunderstand the nature
of the power that they are describing. Nevertheless, it is undeniably true
that mothers' experience with power involves both wielding power over
others (particularly children) and empowering self and others; after all,
the relationship between a mother and child, which serves as the paradigm case for this understanding of power, is exceedingly complex.[69]
Hence, Wartenberg's critique does signal the need for those who accept
this conception of power to develop a more complex and nuanced understanding of the relationship between power-over and empowerment and
of the ways that these two uses of power are intertwined in the experience of mothering.

This lack of attention to the relationship between domination and empowerment gives rise to a further difficulty with the view of power under consideration. The conception of power as empowerment is derived
from an account of "feminine" practices and traits that, at least in large
part, have been constituted as feminine by misogynist cultures. In other
words, at least part of the reason that women are more concerned with
relationships and with empowering and transforming others through relationships is that women have traditionally been told we ought to concern ourselves with these things. This kind of worry has prompted some
feminists to question the claim that women are predisposed to being
more concerned with care, nurturing, and relationships, as opposed to
being concerned with universal justice and autonomy. For instance, Okin
argues that "there is certainly no evidence—nor could there be, in such a
gender-structured society—for concluding that women are somehow
naturally more inclined toward contextuality and away from universal-
ism in their moral thinking, a false concept that unfortunately reinforces
the old stereotypes that justify separate spheres."[70] In Okin's view, there
is no way to know whether women are more concerned with care and relationships because that is woman's nature, or because that is how our
gender has been socially and culturally constructed. She maintains that
empowerment theorists make the mistake of assuming a derivation from
nature, when a derivation from social construction seems at least as
likely, if not more so.

However, this criticism does not stick to the empowerment theorists
that I have been examining. For example, by focusing on the *practice* of
mothering, a practice in which many women engage, Ruddick and Held
clearly avoid making any claims whatsoever about woman's nature. On

the contrary, they base their version of empowerment theory on a set of practices that they acknowledge have been socially constructed. However, a similar problem arises: These empowerment theorists valorize a practice that has taken shape within the context of women's subordination. Although we do not have to go so far as to agree with MacKinnon that to affirm such practices "means to affirm the qualities and characteristics of powerlessness,"[71] it seems quite plausible that such practices have, at best, mixed implications. That is to say, though some aspects of them have been forged by women's own goals and desires, other deeply entwined aspects have been determined by the atmosphere of male dominance in which they have taken shape. This does not mean that such practices cannot have any revolutionary or transformative potential. It does mean that we need to try carefully to disentangle the effects of domination and the products of women's agency in those practices.

To put the point another way, empowerment theorists seem to lose sight of the ways in which the transforming and empowering practices in which they are interested are themselves shaped by relations of domination. This means that these practices are, as Bat-Ami Bar On puts it, "necessarily tainted by oppression."[72] This is not to say that caring, nurturing, and mothering are wholly determined by the subordination of women; women have of course played an important and active role in defining these practices and orienting ourselves to them. Nevertheless, it seems problematic for feminists to valorize and label *as feminist* practices that have been defined within the context of—and, in some cases, designed to uphold—male dominance. Simply to place a positive value on these practices, while simultaneously juxtaposing the resulting conception of power with the "male" conception of power as domination, is to leave these complex problems unresolved. Unlike the view that equates power with domination, which concentrates so much on domination that it fails to recognize women's empowerment as an exercise of power, this conception of power concentrates so much on empowerment that it fails to analyze sufficiently the fact that practices that are empowering to women are developed in and through a dialectical relationship with male domination.

Conclusion

Although the conceptions of power as domination and power as empowerment successfully avoid some of the problems that plagued the power-as-resource model—in particular, the assumption that power is a good or resource that can be possessed, distributed, and redistributed—they give rise to a new problem: Each overemphasizes one aspect of power. Thus, these conceptions of power are not so much wrong as they are incomplete. But, one might wonder, why is the one-sidedness of these conceptions problematic? Perhaps those who understand power as domination and those who understand it as empowerment could just insist that they are talking about different things and leave it at that. The former are examining how male dominance works, and the latter are trying to uncover resources that will enable us to move beyond it. If they simply are talking about different things, then it might make no difference that they come up with different understandings of power. Indeed, we might *expect* them to have different understandings of power, given the differences in their projects.

The one-sidedness of these conceptions of power is problematic for two reasons. First, looking only at one of these aspects of power at a time—*either* the dominating power that men exercise over women *or* the empowering power that women experience—obscures the other forms of domination and subordination that are intertwined with women's subordination.[73] To say that the power that grows out of women's experience is positive, creative, and empowering is to ignore the fact that some women exercise power by dominating others. To claim that women are powerless as such, as domination theorists do, is likewise to blind oneself to the power that some women are able to exercise over others. Women's use of power is not necessarily benevolent; women are not incapable of or unwilling to use our power to hurt others simply because we are women. Many women have access to and exercise power over other women by virtue of their relations to those other women—relations that include race, class, and sexual orientation. Conceptions of power that have a one-sided focus either on male domination or female empowerment miss the ways in which some women play integral roles in the subordination of others, and in which different women are differently empowered by particular practices. To make sense of these phenomena, feminists need a varied, nuanced conception of power that overcomes such conceptual one-sidedness.

Second, a one-sided approach renders each conception of power incapable of making sense of the complex and multifarious power relations in which women find ourselves, which are such that we can be both dominated and empowered at the same time and in the context of one and the same norm, institution, and practice. Mothers, for example, can experience empowerment through the practice of transforming, nurturing, and empowering their children, while at the same time being subject to the power of male domination, in the guise of a male-dominated medical profession, oppressive or abusive husbands, and/or structural disadvantage in the labor market and political sphere; moreover, their experience of motherhood as empowering can plausibly be explained in terms of their relative lack of power in other arenas of their lives.[74] Because their view of power implies that female power is a contradiction in terms, domination theorists fail to see the power that women have as mothers as power. Although empowerment theorists recognize that mothers are socially powerless, they fail to comprehend the full effects of male dominance on their understanding of women's empowerment. Because each of these conceptions is partially blind to the significance of the other, each is incapable of fully illuminating women's complex experience with power.

Feminists have been right to move beyond the liberal conception of power as resource, but we haven't yet gone far enough. It is not enough for feminists to investigate only one of the faces of power—its dominating face or its empowering one—and leave it at that. To do so inevitably distorts our understanding of the face that we choose to examine. Feminists need a conception of power that will illuminate the interplay between domination and empowerment; only such a conception will be conceptually complex enough to illuminate the multifarious relations of power that feminists seek both to critique and to transform. I shall argue in the next two chapters that the analysis of power developed by Michel Foucault and extended by Judith Butler can provide feminists with the resources for developing such a conception.

Notes

1. John Stuart Mill, *The Subjection of Women* (Mineola, N.Y.: Dover, 1997).

2. Susan Moller Okin, *Justice, Gender, and the Family* (New York: Basic Books, 1989).

3. Indeed, in an earlier work, Okin criticizes Mill for believing that the preservation of the traditional gender-structured family is consistent with the full emancipation of women. On this point, see Susan Moller Okin, *Women in Western Political Thought* (Princeton: Princeton University Press, 1979), pp. 226–230.

4. Okin, *Justice, Gender, and the Family*, p. 136.

5. Ibid., p. 170.

6. Ibid., p. 168.

7. Iris Marion Young, *Justice and the Politics of Difference* (Princeton: Princeton University Press, 1990), p. 31.

8. Ibid.

9. Ibid.

10. Ibid. This criticism does not seem to apply to Okin's version of the power-as-resource model, since she gives a very sophisticated account of the structural and institutional features of social and political life that impact on the distribution of power in the family. Thus, Young's claim that this is a feature of distributive models of power per se may be too strong. It is, however, a fair criticism of Mill, who explicitly characterizes the subordination of women as a muted and softened form of slavery. (See Mill, *The Subjection of Women*, p. 5.)

11. Ibid., p. 32.

12. Ibid.

13. Anna Yeatman, "Feminism and Power," in Mary Shanley and Uma Narayan, eds., *Reconstructing Political Theory: Feminist Perspectives* (University Park: Pennsylvania State Press, 1997), p. 144.

14. Catharine MacKinnon, *Feminism Unmodified* (Cambridge, Mass.: Harvard University Press, 1987), p. 34; emphasis MacKinnon's.

15. See Catharine MacKinnon, *Toward a Feminist Theory of the State* (Cambridge, Mass.: Harvard University Press, 1989), p. 238.

16. MacKinnon, *Toward a Feminist Theory of the State*, p. 219.

17. MacKinnon, *Feminism Unmodified*, p. 37.

18. Ibid., p. 220.

19. Ibid., p. 123; emphasis MacKinnon's.

20. Carole Pateman, *The Sexual Contract* (Stanford: Stanford University Press, 1988), p. 207.

21. Pateman, *Sexual Contract*, p. 219.

22. Ibid., p. 158.

23. Ibid., p. 20.

24. MacKinnon, *Toward a Feminist Theory of the State*, pp. 104–105.

25. Andrea Dworkin, *Intercourse* (New York: Free Press, 1987), pp. 125–126; emphasis added and taken away.

26. Nancy Fraser, "Beyond the Master/Subject Model: Reflections on Carole Pateman's *Sexual Contract*," *Social Text* 37 (1993): 173.

27. Pateman, *Sexual Contract*, p. 37.

28. Ibid., p. 2.

29. See ibid., p. 182.

30. Fraser, "Master/Subject," p. 173.

31. MacKinnon, *Feminism Unmodified*, p. 3.

32. Dworkin, *Intercourse*, p. 63; emphasis added.

33. Andrea Dworkin, *Pornography: Men Possessing Women* (New York: Plume, 1979), p. xxxvii. Consider also MacKinnon's claim about Phyllis Schlafly: "I'm saying her analysis of her own experience is wrong. Their foot is on her neck, too, and I, for one, am willing to give her this chance to change her mind" (MacKinnon, *Feminism Unmodified*, p. 30); and her remark, referring to Carol Gilligan's claim that women speak "in a different voice" when it comes to ethical and moral choices: "Take your foot off our necks, then we will hear in what tongue women speak" (MacKinnon, *Feminism Unmodified*, p. 45).

34. Fraser, "Master/Subject," p. 180.

35. Elizabeth Spelman, *Inessential Woman: Problems of Exclusion in Feminist Thought* (Boston: Beacon, 1988), p. 186.

36. Ibid.

37. MacKinnon, *Feminism Unmodified*, p. 53.

38. Pateman, *Sexual Contract*, p. 15.

39. MacKinnon, *Feminism Unmodified*, p. 9; emphasis added.

40. Yeatman, "Feminism and Power," p. 147.

41. As influential as Gilligan's work has been, it is important to note that subsequent studies have failed to vindicate completely her thesis about moral development and gender. See, for example, the works cited in Okin, *Justice, Gender, and*

the Family, pp. 188–189, note 29; and by Jane Mansbridge, "Feminism and Democratic Community," in John Chapman and Ian Shapiro, eds., *Democratic Community: NOMOS XXXV* (New York: New York University Press, 1993), pp. 381–382, note 32.

42. Carol Gilligan, *In a Different Voice: Psychological Theory and Women's Development* (Cambridge, Mass.: Harvard University Press, 1982), p. 22.

43. Sara Ruddick, *Maternal Thinking: Toward a Politics of Peace* (New York: Ballantine, 1989), p. 17; and Virginia Held, *Feminist Morality: Transforming Culture, Society, and Politics* (Chicago: University of Chicago Press, 1993), pp. 197–198.

44. Jean Baker Miller, "Women and Power," in Thomas Wartenberg, ed., *Rethinking Power* (Albany: SUNY Press, 1992), p. 241.

45. Gilligan, *Different Voice,* p. 93.

46. Ibid., p. 114.

47. Held, *Feminist Morality,* p. 137.

48. Ibid., p. 136.

49. Starhawk, *Truth or Dare: Encounters with Power, Authority, and Mystery* (San Francisco: Harper, 1987), p. 8. See also Sarah Lucia Hoagland, *Lesbian Ethics: Toward New Value* (Palo Alto, Calif.: Institute of Lesbian Studies, 1988), p. 117.

50. Hoagland, *Lesbian Ethics,* p. 114.

51. See ibid.

52. Miller, "Women and Power," p. 241. Earlier, she had defined power as "the capacity to implement" (see Jean Baker Miller, *Toward a New Psychology of Women,* 2nd ed. [Boston: Beacon, 1986], p. 116).

53. Ruddick, *Maternal Thinking,* p. 37.

54. Hoagland, *Lesbian Ethics,* p. 118.

55. Hélène Cixous, "Entrieten avec Françoise van Rossum-Guyon," *Revue des sciences humaines* 168 (octobre-décembre 1977): 483–484. Translation mine.

56. Held, *Feminist Morality,* p. 209.

57. Miller, "Women and Power," pp. 247–248.

58. Luce Irigaray, "The Power of Discourse and the Subordination of the Feminine," in Irigaray, *This Sex Which Is Not One,* trans. Catherine Porter (Ithaca: Cornell University Press, 1985), p. 81.

59. Ibid.

60. See Luce Irigaray, "And the One Doesn't Stir Without the Other," trans. Hélène Vivienne Wenzel, *Signs* 7:1 (1981): 60–67; and Eléanor H. Kuykendall, "Toward an Ethic of Nurturance: Luce Irigaray on Mothering and Power," in Joyce Trebilcot, ed., *Mothering: Essays in Feminist Theory* (Savage, Md.: Rowman and Littlefield, 1983).

61. Here I am very much indebted to Thomas Wartenberg's excellent account of the transformative power in *The Forms of Power: From Domination to Transformation* (Philadelphia: Temple University Press, 1990), ch. 9.

62. Wartenberg, *Forms of Power,* p. 191. For an account of Irigaray's focus on transformative power, see Kuykendall, "Toward an Ethic of Nurturance: Luce Irigaray on Mothering and Power."

63. Wartenberg, *Forms of Power,* p. 187.

64. Ibid.

65. Ibid.; emphasis Wartenberg's.

66. Ibid., p. 26.

67. See ibid, p. 23.

68. Ibid., p. 189.

69. As Wartenberg notes (see ibid., p. 198), Ruddick's account does a better job than most of paying attention to the complexity of mothers' experience of power. For instance, although Ruddick sees in mothering the model for a transformative use of power, she also is quick to acknowledge that "mothers have their dominating moments (to understate the case!). . . . Most mothers also know what it is to be dominated" (see Sara Ruddick, "Remarks on the Sexual Politics of Reason," in Eva Feder Kittay and Diana T. Meyers, eds., *Women and Moral Theory* [Lanham, Md.: Rowman and Littlefield, 1987], p. 254).

70. Okin, *Justice, Gender, and the Family*, p. 15.

71. MacKinnon, *Feminism Unmodified*, p. 39.

72. Bat-Ami Bar On, "Marginality and Epistemic Privilege," in Linda Alcoff and Elizabeth Potter, eds., *Feminist Epistemologies* (New York: Routledge, 1993), p. 94.

73. On this point, see Spelman, *Inessential Woman*, pp. 140–141.

74. Okin argues further that women are disadvantaged by the very *anticipation* of motherhood. Recognizing that motherhood and highly demanding careers do not mix well, girls who expect to be mothers at some point in their lives lower their career expectations. (See Okin, *Justice, Gender, and the Family*, pp. 142ff.)

2

The Genealogy of Power: Michel Foucault

Michel Foucault is perhaps best known for his brilliant analysis of power. His genealogical studies of punishment and of sexuality, taken together with interviews given and essays written in the mid-1970s, develop a highly original analysis that challenges and supplants the view of power presupposed by traditional social and political theory. Whereas traditional views take power to be essentially negative, to function always by saying "no," Foucault views power as productive—indeed, as producing the very subjects that it controls. Whereas traditional accounts understand power on the model of the rule of law and take the exercise of the power of the sovereign over his citizens as the paradigm case of a power relation, Foucault rejects this command-obedience model[1] and takes as his paradigm case the minute, diverse, and multifaceted tactical struggle that is carried out at the margins of society. Traditional theories, Foucault complains, define power "in a strangely restrictive way, in that, to begin with, this power is poor in resources, sparing of its methods, monotonous in the tactics it utilizes, incapable of invention, and seemingly doomed always to repeat itself."[2] Foucault, by contrast, views power in a uniquely expansive way; power, for Foucault, is rich in resources, lavish in its methods, varied in its utilization of tactics, and highly inventive in its methods of mobilization.

This way of thinking about power has yielded some very impressive results. With it, Foucault has provided a compelling alternative to liberal conceptions that view power as concentrated in the hands of the sovereign or state, Marxist conceptions that understand power as rooted in the political economy, conceptions based in ideology critique that assume that power is a function of people's beliefs, and liberationist conceptions that view power as essentially repressive. However, despite these theoretical gains, Foucault's analysis of power has come under heavy criticism from political theorists who decry its cryptonormativity, its anarchism, its nihilism, its functionalism, and its denial of subjectivity and agency.[3] Some of these criticisms have been echoed by feminist theorists.[4] In this chapter, I shall argue that, these critiques of Foucault notwithstanding, his account provides some crucial theoretical resources for the development of a feminist conception of power.

I proceed in the first section by laying out some key features of Foucault's conception of power. In the second section, I begin to consider the relationship between this conception of power and feminist theory by considering and responding to some of the most important criticisms that feminists have leveled against Foucault. I maintain that many of these criticisms rest on misunderstandings of Foucault's work and, thus, fall wide of their mark. Moreover, the criticisms that do hit their mark do not warrant a wholesale dismissal of Foucault's analysis of power but, instead, indicate the necessity of supplementing and extending some of Foucault's insights in order to incorporate them into a feminist conception of power. In the third section, I discuss some of the fruitful ways in which feminists have appropriated Foucault's analysis of power and suggest further ways in which that analysis can prove useful for a feminist account of power. In the fourth section, I address the principal problems in Foucault's analysis of power that a feminist appropriation of his work will have to overcome. These limits to the feminist collaboration with Foucault[5] are the result of three lingering problems in his analysis of power: the problem of resistance, the problem of agency, and the problem of solidarity. I conclude by attempting to offer a balanced assessment of the strengths and weaknesses that characterize Foucault's approach to the study of power. I maintain that, despite the limits to the feminist collaboration with Foucault, his work provides key resources for a feminist conception of power.

In making this argument, I shall be suggesting that we should take what is useful in Foucault's analysis, modify it to suit our purposes, reject those aspects that cannot be modified, and incorporate the insights gained into a feminist conception of power. To those who might object to this sort of pragmatic approach on the grounds that it is unfaithful to Foucault's philosophical position, I offer the following statement that Foucault himself once made about Nietzsche: "I prefer to utilise the writers I like. The only valid tribute to thought such as Nietzsche's is precisely to use it, to deform it, to make it groan and protest. And if commentators say that I am being faithful or unfaithful to Nietzsche, that is of absolutely no interest."[6] In this chapter, I point out ways in which feminists might utilize Foucault's analysis of power, certainly make it groan a bit, perhaps even deform it. This, I think, is the only valid tribute to thought such as Foucault's.

Foucault's Conception of Power

In the works of his middle period, power replaces knowledge as the primary lens through which Foucault views the social world. Foucault's genealogical works of the mid-1970s analyze the emergence of specific techniques of power in certain domains of social life that are particular to the modern era. Thus, for example, *Discipline and Punish: The Birth of the Prison*[7] explores the rise of a peculiarly modern modality of power—namely, disciplinary power—in myriad social institutions, including prisons, schools, hospitals, and factories. Similarly, volume 1 of *The History of Sexuality* investigates the rise in the realm of sexuality of a modality of power that is not merely repressive but is also inherently productive, that produces discourses of sexuality even as it attempts to repress them. This insight marks Foucault's analysis as unique, since many theoretical approaches to power (for instance, Freudian, Marxist, or other liberationist approaches) accept the truth of what he labels the "repressive hypothesis"[8]—namely, the view that power is always and only repressive, that it can only say "no." The analysis of power as both repressive and productive is especially evident in Foucault's account of the process of subjection (*assujettisement*). According to Foucault, power subjects individuals in both senses of the term: Individuals are both *subject to* the constraints of social relations of power and simultaneously enabled to take up the position of *a subject* in and through those very constraints. Each of Foucault's genealogical works points to a uniquely modern modality of power, one that differs from previous modalities in that it is capillary, local, and spread throughout the social body, rather than concentrated in the center of the state in the person of the sovereign. In what follows, I shall trace out the general contours of Foucault's conception of power as it emerges from his genealogical analysis.

Foucault's genealogies are guided by his belief that an analysis of power should focus on "power at its extremities, in its ultimate destinations, with those points where it becomes capillary, that is, in its more regional and local forms and institutions."[9] In short, Foucaultian genealogy endeavors to offer a "micro-physics" of modern techniques of power.[10] These methodological exhortations stem from Foucault's belief that modern power operates locally, circulates in the regional and local institutions of the social body, and emanates from every point in the social field. Such modern techniques are in sharp contrast to premodern techniques of power, which, Foucault claims, located power centrally in the sovereign. Whereas premodern power was vested in the particular people or institutions associated with sovereignty, modern power is present in all social relations. It is this feature of modern power that motivates Foucault's genealogical investigations into what might seem to be peripheral social institutions, such as factories, prisons, clinics, schools, and barracks. By targeting such local institutions, Foucault's analysis uncovers power relations that cut across diverse segments of society. In short, his genealogical analysis reveals specific power relations at the level of the everyday.

Perhaps the most striking aspect of Foucault's genealogical analysis of power is his rejection of the belief that power is solely or primarily repressive. Foucault insists that power could not possibly be continually effective if it functioned only by saying "no." As he writes, "If power . . . never did anything but to say no, do you really think one would be brought to obey it?"[11] Although the critique of the "repressive hypothesis" is found in his genealogy of sexuality, the view of power as productive rather than merely repressive is evident in Foucault's genealogy of modern, disciplinary power as well. Thus, at the outset of *Discipline and Punish*, Foucault offers the following as one of the rules that govern his study of disciplinary power: "Do not concentrate the study of the punitive mechanisms on their 'repressive' effects alone, on their 'punishment' aspects alone, but situate them in a whole series of their possible positive effects."[12]

In Foucault's view, the problem with the repressive model is that it does not give power enough credit; power is much more inventive and complex than this model understands or acknowledges. Thus, Foucault characterizes his resolution to study both the repressive and positive effects of disciplinary power as part and parcel of regarding the power of punishment as "a complex social function."[13] In order to understand fully such complex social functions as punishment and the production of sexuality, Foucault claims that "we must cease once and for all to describe the effects of power in negative terms: it 'excludes,' it 'represses,' it 'censors,' it 'abstracts,' it 'masks,' it 'conceals.' In fact, power produces; it produces reality; it produces domains of objects and rituals of truth."[14] In Foucault's view, rather than merely functioning negatively by repressing or prohibiting, power functions positively and productively: It creates objects of analysis, forms discourses that serve as analytical tools, and constructs knowledge. Rather than simply prohibiting, censuring, and restricting, power incites, provokes, and induces.

It may seem from this characterization that Foucault rejects the repressive model of power *tout court*; after all, in the passage just cited he maintains that "we must cease once and for all to describe the effects of power in negative terms." However, I do not think that one can make sense of Foucault's analysis of power as a wholesale rejection of the repressive model of power. On the contrary, in his analysis, productive power often functions repressively, just as repressive power often functions productively. For example, in *Discipline and Punish*, although disciplinary power is productive in that it produces, for instance, delinquents, such delinquents are produced only in and through the operation of the punitive, repressive power of the state. Foucault writes:

> One should not see in delinquency the most intense, most harmful form of illegality . . . ; it is rather an effect of penality . . . that makes it possible to differentiate, accommodate, and supervise illegalities. No doubt delinquency is a form of illegality; certainly it has its roots in illegality; but it is an illegality that the "carceral system" . . . has invested, segmented, isolated, penetrated, organized, enclosed in a definite milieu. . . . For the observation that prison fails to eliminate crime, one should perhaps substitute the hypothesis that prison has succeeded extremely well in producing delinquency.[15]

Thus, disciplinary power is productive insofar as it produces the category of delinquency and incites prisoners to take up their positions as delinquents, but it is able to do so only by mobilizing the repressive power of the state to define illegalities and punish offenders.

This interrelation between the productive and repressive aspects of power is likewise evident in Foucault's description of the rise of "bio-power" in the first volume of *The History of Sexuality*. According to Foucault, in the classical era, the sovereign wielded the "power of life and death" over his people.[16] "Power in this instance was essentially a right of seizure: of things, time, bodies, and ultimately life itself; it culminated in the privilege to seize hold of life in order to suppress it."[17] In the contemporary era, however, power as the right of death exists side by side with a positive, "life-administering" power, a power that "exerts a positive influence on life, that endeavors to administer, optimize, and multiply it, subjecting it to precise controls and comprehensive regulations."[18] As the many bloody wars of this century prove, repressive sovereign power crystallized in the right to claim the lives of subjects is still exercised; however, such power is now coupled with the seamy underside of a productive bio-power that fosters and administers the life and health of the population. According to Foucault, repressive power is intertwined with productive power, and vice versa.

In the introduction to volume 1 of *The History of Sexuality*, Foucault acknowledges the ways that repressive and productive power are complexly intertwined. Although one might think that Foucault's critique of the repressive hypothesis leads him to reject the claim that power prohibits certain forms of sexuality, Foucault insists otherwise:

> I do not maintain that the prohibition of sex is a ruse; but it is a ruse to make prohibition into the basic and constitutive element from which one would be able to write the history of what has been said concerning sex starting from the modern epoch. All these negative elements—defenses, censorships, denials—. . . are doubtless only component parts that have a local and tacti-

cal role to play in . . . a technology of power . . . that [is] far from being re-
ducible to the former.[19]

Given this acknowledgment that productive and repressive power are interrelated—indeed, that repressive power often serves the interests of
productive power—Foucault resolves to search "for instances . . . of the
production of power (which sometimes have the function of prohibiting)."[20] Despite his rhetoric, which sometimes suggests a wholesale rejection of any understanding of power as repressive or prohibitive, for Foucault, power *both* prohibits *and* produces; indeed, it prohibits by
producing, and it produces by prohibiting. As Judith Butler puts the
point, for Foucault, "production . . . is at the same time constraint."[21]

For Foucault, one of the key effects of this prohibitive/productive
power is the "subject," a claim for which he is famous—or infamous, depending on your perspective.[22] In Foucault's analysis, subjection (*assujettisement*) has a double meaning: First, it connotes the fact that one is *subject to* a power that is being exercised over one; second and
simultaneously, it refers to the fact that one is able to take up the position
of *a subject* only in and through this operation of power. In this way,
power's productive and repressive aspects are intertwined with respect
to the subject; power both enables the constitution of subjects and constrains the options of those subjects at the same time.

Foucault's genealogy of disciplinary power illuminates this dual
meaning of subjection. This genealogy traces the process by which individuals are subjected to normalizing disciplinary practices and thereby
transformed into a certain kind of subject—namely, a docile body. As
Foucault says, "Discipline 'makes' individuals; it is the specific technique
of a power that regards individuals both as objects and as instruments of
its exercise."[23] In other words, individuals are subject to disciplinary
power, which is exercised over them and subtly and insidiously constrains their available options. At the same time, individuals are enabled
to take up the position of a social, discursive, and political subject by disciplinary power, which creates various subject-positions and incites individuals to take them up. Disciplinary power both enables and constrains
individual subjects; further, it constrains by enabling, and enables only
insofar as it constrains.[24] Similarly, Foucault's genealogy of sexuality illuminates this understanding of subjection. Power operates in and through
the practice of confession both to subject individuals to the injunction to
tell the truth about their sexuality and to enable them to take up the position of sexual subject. For instance, according to Foucault, the practice of
confession incites us to confess our secrets, our desires, our pleasures,
and our darkest thoughts; this injunction "has submitted generations in
order to produce . . . men's subjection: their constitution as subjects in

both senses of the word."[25] Power operating in and through the practice of confession enables and constrains modern subjects; further, it enables by constraining, and it constrains only insofar as it enables.

Foucault's conception of power is thus clearly at odds with the conception of power presupposed by traditional social and political philosophy. Rather than viewing power as a force that is wielded by the state to prohibit certain actions on the part of autonomous and self-constituted subjects, Foucault understands power as a mobile set of force relations that operate throughout the social body. These force relations both produce and prohibit domains of knowledge, discourses of truth, tools of analysis, and individual subjects; moreover, they produce only insofar as they prohibit, and prohibit by producing. As I shall discuss in the next section, this conception of power has been sharply criticized by some feminists. Before I can make the case that Foucault's analysis is useful for the development of a feminist conception of power, I shall have to consider these criticisms in some detail.

A Theory for Women?

Nancy Hartsock has made the strongest case for the position that Foucault's analysis is not only unhelpful for feminist thinking about power but actually undermines such a project; thus, any attempt to draw on Foucault's analysis of power for feminist purposes must come to grips with Hartsock's trenchant critique. Although Hartsock is willing to grant that Foucault has made a number of important contributions to the study of power, she specifies two related objections to his analysis. First, she maintains that Foucault thinks about power from the perspective of one who is able to exercise power—from the perspective of the colonizer—rather than from the perspective of one who is subjugated—from the perspective of the colonized.[26] Second, since Foucault views power from the perspective of the colonizer and since "domination, viewed from above, is more likely to appear as equality,"[27] Hartsock claims that Foucault's conception of power obscures rather than reveals systematically unequal power relations. On the basis of these two arguments, Hartsock concludes that Foucault's work is "inadequate and even irrelevant to the needs of the colonized or the dominated."[28] I shall consider each of her objections in some detail.

Hartsock begins her critique of Foucault by noting that "Foucault's world is not my world but is instead a world in which I feel profoundly alien. . . . Foucault's is a world in which things move, rather than people, a world in which active subjects become obliterated or, rather, re-created as passive objects, a world in which passivity or refusal represent the only possible choices."[29] Here, Hartsock expresses a worry about Foucault's claim that the subject is an effect of power relations.[30] She implies that such a critique necessitates a view of the subject as passive and impotent. Indeed, Hartsock suggests that such a thoroughgoing critique of the subject at this particular moment in history plays a bit too conveniently into the hands of those in a position of dominance; thus, she asks, "Why is it that just at the moment when so many of us who have been silenced begin to demand the right to name ourselves, to act as subjects rather than objects of history, that just then the concept of subjecthood becomes problematic?"[31] In Hartsock's view, Foucault's critique of the subject serves to undercut the demands of marginalized and oppressed peoples to attain the status of subjects, a status from which they have been systematically excluded throughout history. As a result, Foucault's thinking is on the side of the colonizers rather than the colonized; it is "with" power rather than "against" it.[32]

Hartsock sees further evidence for Foucault's collusion with power in his account of subjugated knowledges. She cites Foucault's claim that subjugated knowledges are "not allowed to function within official knowledge"[33] and his characterizations of such knowledges as "insurrectionary," "disordered," and "fragmentary."[34] Hartsock maintains that subjugated knowledges could appear to be illegitimate only if they are viewed from the perspective of official knowledges—that is, from the perspective of those in power. Since Foucault characterizes such knowledges as illegitimate, he must be thinking of them from the perspective of the powerful colonizers. Furthermore, Hartsock indicates that it is Foucault's colonizing perspective that leads him to offer an unsatisfactory account of the possibilities of opposition on the part of subjugated knowledges to official power/knowledge regimes. Hartsock finds this account unsatisfactory both because it focuses on mere resistance to power rather than more radical transformation of power relations and because its understanding of such resistance is too vague. Accordingly, Hartsock concludes that

> Foucault, . . . despite his stated aims of producing an account of power that will enable and facilitate resistance and opposition, instead adopts the position of what he has termed official knowledge with regard to the knowledge of the dominated and reinforces the relations of domination in our society by insisting that those of us who have been marginalized in various ways remain at the margins.[35]

It seems to me that Hartsock's claim that Foucault obliterates the subject or turns active subjects into passive objects is based on a misunderstanding of his project. Hartsock takes Foucault to be offering a substantive critique of the very notion of subjectivity. It is undoubtedly true that

Foucault writes subjects out of his genealogies, but this is a methodological move that is designed to displace a particular conception of the subject—namely, the humanist conception—and not to undermine the very concept of subjectivity itself.[36] As Foucault puts the point in an interview conducted in 1971: "The theory of the subject (in the double sense of the word) is at the heart of humanism and this is why our culture has tenaciously rejected anything that could weaken its hold upon us. But it can be attacked in two ways: either by a 'desubjectification' of the will to power . . . or by the destruction of the subject as pseudosovereign."[37] This statement is quite illuminating. First, it suggests that Foucault's method of writing the subject out of his analysis of power has a very particular purpose—namely, to unseat a humanist theory of the subject and, by extension, to weaken the hold of humanism itself. Second, it indicates that Foucault's obliteration of the subject is really aimed at a particular conception of the subject—"the subject as pseudosovereign"—and not at the concept of subjectivity per se. These considerations suggest that Foucault's inattention to subjectivity can be read as a kind of bracketing of the question of subjectivity, a bracketing that is designed to undermine the humanist conception and, thus, to clear the ground for alternate conceptions of subjectivity.[38]

Thus, I think Hartsock's charge that Foucault turns all subjects into passive objects and, thus, eradicates the subject itself is too strong. Nevertheless, there is an element of truth in this critique. Although I would defend Foucault against the extreme claim that he eradicates the subject, I would not deny that there are real problems with Foucault's account of subjectivity, particularly with the view of agency that it implies. I shall discuss these problems in more detail below. However, I shall maintain that these problems do not necessitate the wholesale rejection of a Foucaultian-feminism; indeed, as I argue in Chapter 3, Judith Butler's recent work, which adopts a Foucaultian-feminist framework for the study of power, is able to overcome the paradox of agency in which Foucault's own analysis of power remains mired.

Similarly, Hartsock's objection to Foucault's characterization of subjugated knowledges strikes me as too hasty. She maintains that such knowledges could appear to be illegitimate only from the perspective of the dominant power-knowledge regime; thus, if Foucault characterizes these knowledges as illegitimate, then he must be viewing them from a position of dominance. However, it seems to me that Foucault's claim is precisely that subjugated knowledges only *appear* to be illegitimate *when viewed from the perspective of* the official power-knowledge regime. Indeed, insofar as the official power-knowledge regime of a society defines and determines what counts as legitimacy and illegitimacy, it seems inevitable that subjugated knowledges would be characterized as illegiti-

mate by the dominant knowledge. I don't see how Hartsock could disagree with this point, since it seems to be simply an elaboration of what it
means to say that a knowledge is subjugated. Foucault's presentation of
this state of affairs doesn't necessarily imply that this is how he himself
views subjugated knowledges. Subjugated knowledges, for Foucault, are
knowledges that *"have been disqualified* as inadequate to their task or insufficiently elaborated: naive knowledges, located low down on the hierarchy, beneath the required level of cognition or scientificity."[39] Thus,
when viewed from the perspective of dominant knowledge, subjugated
knowledges are illegitimate, disordered, and fragmentary. But this is not
to deny that, when viewed from another perspective, these knowledges
have their own logic, order, and legitimacy. As Foucault says of workers'
knowledges:

> [T]he workers, at the beginning of the nineteenth century, carried out de-
> tailed investigations into their material conditions. This work served Marx
> for the bulk of his documentation; it led, in large part, to the political and
> trade-union practices of the proletariat throughout the nineteenth century; it
> maintains and develops itself through continuing struggles. Yet this knowl-
> edge has never been allowed to function within official knowledge.[40]

Here, Foucault acknowledges that the subjugated knowledge of workers
has its own material bases, its own set of concomitant practices, its own
logic of development; it is only from the perspective of official knowledge that the knowledge of workers has been viewed as inadequate.

However, to claim that Foucault acknowledges that subjugated knowledges have their own internal logic is not to claim that he advocates elevating these knowledges to the level of the dominant power-knowledge
regime of the West—namely, to the level of a unified, theoretical science.
Given Hartsock's historical materialism and her valorization of the
knowledge gleaned through women's experience of oppression, I suspect that it is Foucault's unwillingness to exalt subjugated knowledges to
a position of dominance that Hartsock really rejects. To be sure, the aim
of genealogy is not to develop a new science, premised upon the claims
of these subjugated knowledges, that will disqualify and thus supplant
the official power/knowledge regime. Genealogies are not sciences, they
are "anti-sciences."[41] The aim of genealogies is to take seriously subjugated knowledges and to entertain their claims against those of "a uni-
tary body of theory which would filter, hierarchise and order them in the
name of some true knowledge and some arbitrary idea of what constitutes a science and its objects."[42] Although Hartsock criticizes this as too
anemic an account of resistance, Foucault's position is that to try to turn
subjugated knowledges into sciences would simply be to repeat the very

same problematic that he is diagnosing and would serve to institute a whole new series of repressions and exclusions. If we are interested in elevating a subjugated knowledge to the level of a science, then, Foucault maintains, we must ask ourselves: "[W]hat types of knowledge do you want to disqualify in the very instant of your demand: 'Is it a science'? Which speaking, discoursing subjects . . . do you want to 'diminish' when you say: 'I who conduct this discourse am conducting a scientific discourse, and I am a scientist'?"[43] Thus, Hartsock's charge that Foucault "reinforces the relations of domination in our society by insisting that those of us who have been marginalized in various ways remain at the margins" is misleading. Although Foucault *does* reject the idea that those who have been marginalized should move to the center, he does so only because he rejects the very notion of a center itself. Thus it may be that Foucault wants the marginalized to stay at the margins; but insofar as he also undermines the very notion of a center, this seems to me to be much less problematic than Hartsock assumes.

I suspect that in the end Hartsock's claim that Foucault views power from the perspective of the colonizer boils down to the complaint that Foucault is *unable* to view power in any other way given that he is a white, economically and educationally privileged, Western European man. Indeed, Hartsock's thoroughgoing materialism and her commitment to developing a woman's standpoint in epistemology and conceptualization of power provide indirect evidence for this reading of her critique, even if Hartsock herself never comes out and says as much.[44] If it is the case that Hartsock assumes that Foucault can speak only from the perspective of the colonizer—that is, of one who is powerful—then she seems guilty of ignoring the ways in which Foucault himself was in a subordinate social position because of his sexuality. Unless she is willing to claim that heterosexism does not exist, then it seems that, according to Hartsock's own view, Foucault's experiences as a gay man would position him against power rather than with it. To be sure, these experiences may not be such that it makes sense to understand them in terms of the experiences of the colonized, but I would suggest that this fact only points out the inadequacy of the colonizer/colonized model for making sense of all the complex systematic axes of stratification in contemporary societies; it does not justify the assumption that gay men are not against power.

However, it is not the internal inconsistency of Hartsock's criticism that I find most disturbing. I am most troubled by the idea that feminists can't find useful the theories of white, European men. If this is an implication of her view, it strikes me that this makes the task at hand much more difficult than it need be. I think feminists should be more pragmatic than this. We should make use of the theories of men and of women, of the privileged and the not-so-privileged, to try to construct a theory of power. We should draw on the resources that are offered by existing accounts of power without feeling thereby obliged to take on these theories or the perspectives of their authors whole-hog. Despite its limitations, I shall maintain that Foucault's analysis provides quite useful tools for this kind of feminist approach to the study of power.

Hartsock's second criticism of Foucault is related to her claim that he views power from the perspective of the colonizer rather than from the perspective of the colonized. She writes: "The result of these positions is that power becomes evanescent, and systematic power relations ultimately vanish from his work. This may be related to my first point: domination, viewed from above, is more likely to appear as equality."[45] Hartsock notes Foucault's emphasis on the way that power relations pervade the social body and his use of metaphors such as a net and a web to describe the workings of pervasive social power. In Hartsock's view, three related problems emerge from this kind of understanding of power. First, Foucault's "stress on heterogeneity and the specificity of each situation leads him to lose track of social structures and instead to focus on how individuals experience and exercise power";[46] thus, it seems that if domination is to be located anywhere, it will have to be located in relationships between individuals. However, Foucault also claims that individuals are themselves effects of power, a claim that seems difficult to reconcile with the claim that some individuals exercise domination over others. Thus, "power must not be seen as either a single individual dominating others or as one group or class dominating others."[47] But this, according to Hartsock, amounts to an inability to theorize domination at all, including domination in gender relations.

In addition, Hartsock argues that Foucault's use of the images of net and web to describe power relations "carries implications of equality and participation rather than the systematic domination of the many by the few."[48] If power is a net, we are all equally caught in its strands; but if we are all *equally* caught, then none of us is more responsible than anyone else for the state of things. Hartsock does not stop with claiming that Foucault implies that we are all equally caught in the network of power relations; via a consideration of Foucault's contention that power "comes from below,"[49] she goes on to charge him with insinuating that those who are subjugated are actually *more* responsible for their subjugation than those who are in a position of dominance. Based on her reading of Foucault's use of the image of the net and of the claim that power comes from below, Hartsock concludes that "Foucault's argument for an 'ascending analysis' of power could lead us to engage in blaming the victim."[50]

Finally, Hartsock takes issue with Foucault's assertion that power is capillary and that it operates at the extremities of the social body. This amounts to the claim that power is omnipresent—as Hartsock puts it, "After all, in physical terms, where do we not have capillaries?"[51] The problem with this view is that power starts to look very much like the night in which all cows are black. In Foucault's analysis, Hartsock contends, "power is everywhere, and so ultimately nowhere."[52]

My response to Hartsock's second criticism of Foucault turns on a more sympathetic and, I think, accurate reconstruction of his understanding of power. Hartsock complains that Foucault's emphasis on local power relations leads him to ignore broad, systemic patterns of power distribution. It seems to me, however, that Foucault does not ignore such structural power relations; on the contrary, he is just concerned with *how* one goes about studying such patterns or structures. Again, Hartsock mistakes Foucault's methodological critique of structural analyses of power for a substantive one. He rejects top-down or descending analyses of power—such as the kind of analysis presupposed by traditional Marxism—on the grounds that they are "too glib."[53] The problem with such analyses, according to Foucault, is that "anything can be deduced from the general phenomenon of the domination of the bourgeois class."[54] Here, Foucault wisely cautions us against the not uncommon tendency to find domination wherever we happen to go looking for it. This is why Foucault instead calls for an "ascending analysis of power," an analysis that starts "from its infinitesimal mechanisms, which each have their own history, their own trajectory, their own techniques and tactics, and then see[s] how these mechanisms of power have been—and continue to be—invested, colonised, utilised, involuted, transformed, displaced, extended, etc., by ever more general mechanisms."[55] But the exposure of these "ever more general mechanisms" is nonetheless a goal of genealogical analysis. As Foucault puts it in volume 1 of *The History of Sexuality:*

No "local center," no "pattern of transformation" could function if, through a series of sequences, it did not eventually enter into an over-all strategy. And inversely, no strategy could achieve comprehensive effects if [it] did not gain support from precise and tenuous relations serving, not as its point of application or final outcome, but as its prop and anchor point.[56]

In light of this claim, Hartsock's worry that Foucault ignores the ways in which local, particular power relations are integrated into patterns of power distribution that cut across temporal, institutional, and contextual barriers seems unfounded.[57]

However, this response doesn't counter Hartsock's claim that Foucault's analysis of power is blind to relations of *domination*. After all, Foucault does not generally characterize the ever more general mechanisms of power of which he speaks as instances of systemic patterns of domination. But it seems unfair for Hartsock to criticize Foucault for being blind to relations of domination given that she ignores the way that Foucault draws a distinction between power and domination in one of his late interviews. There, Foucault claims that power relations—both at the local level and at the most general levels—are always variable and unstable; these easily mutable kinds of power relations are contrasted with

> states of domination, in which the relations of power, instead of being variable and allowing different partners a strategy which alters them, find themselves firmly set or congealed. When an individual or a social group manages to block a field of relations of power, to render them impassive and invariable and to prevent all reversibility of movement—by means of instruments which can be economic as well as political or military—we are facing what can be called a state of domination.[58]

According to Foucault, then, in a state of domination the loose network of power relations in which power is supposed to circulate freely is "congealed," so that power cannot circulate to some parts of the social body. Foucault believes that power is an unavoidable element of social life. Thus, any vision of the good society must account for the presence of power relations, and all social critics must remain vigilant with respect to the way such relations are constituted in a particular culture. However, it is not the presence of power per se, but rather the lack of a free flow of power, that Foucault finds objectionable.[59] For this reason, he has claimed that we should not struggle for a society in which there is no power—for this is, in his view, impossible; instead, we should struggle for a society in which there is no, or very little, domination.

To be sure, this characterization of domination is not without its problems. On the one hand, Foucault claims, there are networks of power relations that are unstable, variable, and easily mutable and through which power circulates freely. On the other hand, there are states of domination, in which power does not circulate at all; rather, it flows in only one direction, such that some individuals are left completely unable to exercise it. Admittedly, neither of these options seems completely adequate for a feminist analysis of domination. For although it is certainly true in some instances that the power relations within which women are situated prove to be reversible and unstable, sadly this is not always the case. Similarly, although we would expect that the systematic disadvantage of women would be a "state of domination" in Foucault's sense of the term, it does not seem accurate to follow Foucault in saying that because women are subordinate, the power relations in which we are caught are "impassive and invariable and ... prevent all reversibility of move-ment." Rather, sometimes the domination relations in which we find our-selves prove to be reversible, and sometimes they do not. Foucault's claim that in a state of domination the network of power relations is *congealed* thus seems too strong; instead, I would suggest that in such states, power networks are *constricted*, so that the range of options that are avail-able for those in subordinate positions to exercise power is limited. This way of characterizing domination has the advantage of being more in keeping with the analysis, discussed above, of the interplay between con-straint and enablement that Foucault develops in his genealogies. Thus, Foucault does offer a way of distinguishing between power and domina-tion that, even if it is not completely adequate as it stands, can easily be reformulated to be consistent with the spirit of the bulk of his writings about power.

The second part of Hartsock's criticism of Foucault on this point strikes me as self-contradictory. It seems impossible for Foucault be guilty at the same time *both* of claiming that everyone is equally responsible for power relations *and* of blaming the victim. However, setting this internal incon-sistency aside for the moment, if you take seriously Foucault's discussion of domination as the congealing—or, as I have reformulated his point, the constricting—of networks of power, then he does not seem guilty of claiming that everyone is equally responsible for the state of power rela-tions. Instead, he seems to be suggesting that power flows more freely through some parts of the network than through others. Indeed, even though there is only one occasion (a late interview) on which Foucault explicitly draws the distinction between domination and power, this sug-gestion that power flows more freely through some parts of the social body than through others is consistent with his earlier formulations. For example, he writes, "Everywhere that power exists, it is being exercised. No one, strictly speaking, has an official right to power; and yet it is al-ways exerted in a particular direction, with some people on one side and some on the other. It is often difficult to say who holds power in a precise sense, *but it is easy to see who lacks power*."[60] And if some people clearly lack power, then it cannot be the case that everyone is equally responsi-ble for the existing relations of power. Thus, in the very texts upon which Hartsock bases her interpretation, Foucault cautions against the kind of reading of power that she adopts.

Further, Hartsock's claim that Foucault's analysis of power tends to-ward blaming victims for their fate seems to me to be based on a misun-derstanding. Hartsock bases this criticism on Foucault's claim that power comes from below, which she evidently takes to mean that power comes from those who are in a subordinate position—that is, from those who are on the bottom of the social hierarchy. Thus, she concludes, "[i]t is certainly true that dominated groups participate in their own domination. But rather than stop with the fact of participation, we would learn a great deal more by focusing on the means by which this participation is enacted. Foucault's argument for an 'ascending analysis' of power could lead us to engage in a version of blaming the victim."[61] In the first place, this criticism goes against Hartsock's own interpretation of Foucault; if she is right that Foucault ignores relations of domination, then he can't possibly be claiming that power comes from those who are dominated. If he is really guilty of ignoring domination, then there are simply no victims in his analysis to blame. However, even if we accept my claim that Foucault doesn't ignore the problem of domination, this criticism is still misplaced. The claim that power comes from below is not a claim about power relations between those on the top of the social hierarchy and those on the bottom, between dominant and subordinate individuals; instead, it is a methodological claim about the level at which one should begin one's analysis of power. As I discussed above, Foucault proposed starting at the level of particular power relations in families, institutions, prisons, and so on, and working his way up to "major dominations," which are "the hegemonic effects that are sustained by all these confrontations."[62]

That this methodological precaution does not entail blaming the victim is clear, I think, from one of the examples that Foucault considers by way of an explanation and justification of his approach. He compares the top-down and bottom-up approaches to the study of power with respect to the bourgeoisie's treatment of infantile sexuality. A top-down analysis of power would approach this topic by first claiming that the bourgeoisie is in a position of dominance over the working class; it would then go on to deduce the repression of infantile sexuality from this initial premise. This kind of deduction is easily done and it may even be partially correct, but Foucault thinks it is too easy and, thus, too easily refuted by an alternate sort of top-down investigation. Foucault claims that his ascending analysis, by contrast, involves exploring the ways in which

> these phenomena of repression or exclusion possessed their instruments and their logic, in response to a certain number of needs. We need to identify the agents responsible for them, their real agents (those which constituted the immediate social *entourage*, the family, parents, doctors, etc.), and not be content to lump them under the formula of the generalized bourgeoisie.[63]

Notice that Foucault does not propose beginning with the behavior of the children whose sexuality was monitored and repressed via the interdiction on infantile sexuality; thus, investigating the way that power comes from below clearly does not involve beginning with the actions and behavior of the dominated. Furthermore, Foucault makes it clear that his ascending analysis of power does not let the bourgeoisie off the hook; thus, the upshot of his bottom-up analysis is that what served the bourgeoisie's interests in this historical development was not the repression of infantile sexuality itself but "the techniques and procedures themselves of such an exclusion" that that repression provided.[64] Far from blaming the victims of the bourgeois repression of infantile sexuality, Foucault's approach places responsibility on the bourgeoisie for an even more sinister set of historical developments than those imagined by top-down investigations of power.

Hartsock's final criticism of Foucault's analysis of power—that if power is everywhere, it is ultimately nowhere—seems to me to be the only criticism that really hits its mark. Nancy Fraser has made a similar criticism, but in a potentially more damaging way. Fraser links Foucault's claim that power is everywhere with the claim that it is ineliminable and thus normatively neutral. But given the normative confusions that Fraser diagnoses in Foucault's work, this claim that power is ubiquitous, ineliminable, and normatively neutral is highly problematic. Thus, she concludes,

> Foucault calls too many different sorts of things power and simply leaves it at that. Granted, all cultural practices involve constraints—but these constraints are of a variety of different kinds and thus demand a variety of different normative responses. Granted, there can be no social practices without power—but it doesn't follow that all forms of power are normatively equivalent nor that any social practices are as good as any other.[65]

I think it is true that Foucault is guilty of not making sufficiently fine-grained conceptual and normative distinctions between different uses of power. After all, the only distinction he does make—between power and domination—is made only once in an interview given a few months before his death.[66] However, in my view, this problem in and of itself isn't enough to make Foucault's conception of power not only useless for feminism but also subversive of the aims of feminist theory, as Hartsock contends. It does suggest, however, that if feminists are to put Foucault's conception of power to good use, we shall have to supply such conceptual and normative distinctions and to make sense of his work in light of them.[67] I shall turn to this project in Chapter 5.

Perhaps Hartsock is right in concluding that Foucault's analysis of power is not a theory *for women*. After all, his view has consistently been interpreted as advocating a deconstruction of oppositions, including, but not limited to, the distinction between women and men, rather than a valorization of the heretofore devalued and derided half of such oppositions.[68] However, as I shall argue in the next section, this does not mean that Foucault's analysis of power is not a theory *for feminists*.

A Theory for Feminists

The belief that Foucault's genealogy of power is relevant for feminist theorists is perhaps rooted in a basic similarity between Foucaultian and feminist approaches to the study of power. After all, Foucault's account of the local and capillary nature of modern power clearly resonates with feminist attempts to expand the boundaries of social and political theory to include arenas of life that have heretofore been considered private, natural, and, thus, out of bounds for critique. Nancy Fraser has characterized Foucault's study of power in the following way:

> Foucault enables us to understand power very broadly, and yet very finely, as anchored in the multiplicity of what he calls "micropractices," the social practices that constitute everyday life in modern societies. This positive conception of power has the general but unmistakable implication of a call for a "politics of everyday life."[69]

This description of Foucaultian power echoes the feminist demand that relations and events that were heretofore considered private or personal—and, as such, immune to both the operations of power and the requirements of justice—be recognized as political. For example, feminists placed domestic violence on the social and political agenda by insisting that what had previously been viewed as a series of isolated familial disturbances was actually a widespread abuse of male power in the family that contributed substantially to the disadvantage of women. Like Foucault, they shifted their focus to a set of local power relations that do not take place at the center of the social body, that are not imposed by the state or official economy (which is not to say that they are not regulated, permitted, and/or purposely ignored in the spheres). Feminists insisted on the importance of theorizing a phenomenon that takes place in the periphery of the social body—a set of power relations that emanates from all of the extremities in the social field, that springs up in households throughout society amongst people of varying ethnic, religious, racial and class backgrounds. Foucault's contention that power is at work not just in the state or official economy, but in all arenas of modern social life, echoes feminists' attempts to redefine the scope and bounds of the political. Thus, the feminist insistence that "the personal is political" and the Foucaultian "politics of everyday life" clearly represent complementary forms of analysis.

But let me not be misunderstood. My point here is not that feminists "need" Foucault in order to conduct a microtactical analysis of male domination; many feminists have done and continue to do this kind of analysis just fine without him. However, as I pointed out in Chapter 1, although power is clearly a crucial concept for feminist theory, most feminists have thus far shied away from producing the kind of full-fledged analysis of the concept of power that Foucault presents.[70] My point is that Foucault's theoretical conception of power matches up nicely with the ways in which many feminists have investigated the workings of male power; as a result, his analysis seems useful, at least in this respect, for the task of developing a specifically feminist conception of power.

One of the most fruitful aspects of Foucault's analysis of power for feminist theory has been his account of how disciplinary practices work to shape the body. In *Discipline and Punish*, Foucault discusses the practice of punishment as the focal point for a continually transforming set of power relations that cut across divergent institutional contexts. Disciplinary practices—which include minute regulations of movement, detailed time schedules, and perpetual surveillance—are put to use in a variety of institutions, including the army, the school, the prison, and the factory; these practices shape the bodies of soldiers, students, prisoners and workers into "docile bodies." With the rise of disciplinary power,

> the human body was entering a machinery of power that explores it, breaks it down and rearranges it. . . . [A] "mechanics of power" . . . was being born; it defined how one may have a hold over others' bodies, not only so that they may do what one wishes, but so that they may operate as one wishes, with the techniques, the speed and the efficiency that one determines. Thus discipline produces subjected and practised bodies, "docile" bodies.[71]

Since these various institutions mobilize a similar set of disciplinary practices in the service of creating a set of docile bodies, it is not surprising to Foucault that "prisons resemble factories, schools, barracks, hospitals, which all resemble prisons."[72]

To be sure, Foucault's account of the ways that disciplinary tactics produce docile bodies ignores the differential effect of disciplinary power on women's bodies. This has led Sandra Bartky to wonder: "Where [in Foucault's work] is the account of the disciplinary practices that engender the 'docile bodies' of women, bodies more docile than the bodies of men? Women, like men, are subject to many of the same disciplinary practices Foucault describes. But he is blind to those disciplines that produce a modality of embodiment that is peculiarly feminine."[73] Although Foucault himself fails to give an account of the effects of disciplinary power on women's bodies, Bartky's analysis of this phenomenon is decidedly Foucaultian. She focuses on three practices whose object is the disciplining of the female body: constant dieting aimed at keeping the female

body thin; constriction of gestures and limitation of mobility, which serve
to keep the female body from taking up too much space; and ornamenta-
tion, which makes the female body a pleasant sight.[74] Bartky's analysis of
these disciplinary practices and their effects on women's bodies finds its
inspiration in Foucault's account of the effects of power on the body.[75]

Bartky also draws on Foucault's discussion of the Panopticon to discuss the effects of disciplinary power on women. The Panopticon is a
prison designed with a tower in the center encircled by backlit cells; from
the tower, all of the inmates in their cells are visible, but from the cells, it
is impossible to determine if anyone is actually inside the tower. The
Panopticon functions by convincing prisoners that they may at any given
moment be under surveillance, thereby inducing them to constantly
monitor themselves. As Foucault writes with respect to the inmates in a
Panopticon, "He who is subjected to a field of visibility, and who knows
it, assumes responsibility for the constraints of power; he makes them
play spontaneously upon himself; he inscribes in himself the power relation in which he simultaneously plays both roles; he becomes the principle of his own subjection."[76]

Bartky extends Foucault's analysis by claiming that disciplinary power
likewise compels women to discipline ourselves, to become the principle
of our own subjection. She writes:

> [I]t is women who practice this discipline on and against their own
> bodies. . . . The woman who checks her make-up half a dozen times a day to
> see if her foundation has caked or her mascara has run, who worries that the
> wind or rain may spoil her hairdo, who looks frequently to see if her stock-
> ings have bagged at the ankle, or who, feeling fat, monitors everything she
> eats, has become, just as surely as the inmate of the Panopticon, a self-polic-
> ing subject, a self committed to a relentless self-surveillance. This self-sur-
> veillance is a form of obedience to patriarchy.[77]

In this way, Bartky again makes a convincing case for the relevance of
Foucault's analysis of disciplinary power for feminist theoretical aims,
despite his own lack of concern with the differential effects of such power
on women.

Feminists have also made use of Foucault's analysis of power for a critique of certain institutions in late-capitalist democracies that regulate,
enforce, and maintain the subordination of women. Foucault's genealogical analyses shed light on the role that institutions play in the maintenance of power relations. For example, *Discipline and Punish* not only analyzes the construction of "delinquency" and the practice of discipline, it
also examines the institution of the prison in which these meanings and
practices are embedded.[78] The prison as an institution obeys its own logic

and follows its own principles, and, in so doing, reconstitutes and perpetuates the power that is exercised over the prisoners. Following Foucault, Nancy Fraser and Linda Gordon offer a genealogical analysis of the way the term *dependency* functions in the institutions of welfare states.[79] They write:

> We seek to dispel the *doxa* surrounding current U.S. discussions of dependency by reconstructing that term's genealogy. Modifying an approach associated with Michel Foucault, we will excavate broad historical shifts in linguistic usage that can rarely be attributed to specific agents. We do *not* present a causal analysis. Rather, by contrasting present meanings of dependency with past meanings, we aim to defamiliarize taken-for-granted beliefs in order to render them susceptible to critique and to illuminate present-day conflicts.[80]

This Foucaultian-feminist genealogical project examines the ways in which the institutions of the welfare state produce certain definitions of dependency, associate these definitions with the so-called undeserving poor (predominantly women of color), and thus encourage and perpetuate particular social practices that systematically disadvantage women.[81]

These feminist appropriations and extensions of Foucault's genealogical projects provide good *prima facie* evidence that his analysis is helpful for feminist investigations into the maintenance and functioning of male domination. Moreover, and more important for my task in this book, I would suggest that Foucault's account offers some key resources for the development of a feminist conception of power. For my purposes, the most important of these resources is the ability to view power simultaneously as constraint and enablement and to highlight the complex interplay between the two. As I argued in Chapter 1, feminist discussions of power tend to falter because they overemphasize power understood as dominance and thus have a difficult time adequately accounting for empowerment and resistance, or because they overemphasize empowerment and thus have a difficult time adequately accounting for dominance, or because they fail to highlight the complex interplay between domination and empowerment or resistance and thus end up obscuring both. Foucault's analysis of power, by contrast, highlights the ways in which power both constrains individuals by subjecting them to regulation, control, and normalization and, at the same time, enables or empowers individuals by positioning them as subjects who are endowed with the capacity to act. Foucault characterizes the interplay between these two uses of power in the following passage:

> [The exercise of power] is a total structure of actions brought to bear upon possible actions; it incites, it induces, it seduces, it makes easier or more dif-

ficult; in the extreme it constrains or forbids absolutely; it is nevertheless always a way of acting upon an acting subject or acting subjects by virtue of their acting or being capable of action.[82]

In other words, instances of constraint—that is, exercises of power-over—are, for Foucault, possible only insofar as the subject of the constraint is simultaneously enabled—that is, as a subject who has the capacity to act, who has power-to. Thus, Foucault not only conceptualizes power in terms of both power-over and power-to, he also integrates these two aspects of power in a complex and instructive way.

Thus, Foucault's conceptualization of power allows for the fact that, although power-over and power-to are useful analytical categories, they represent features of social relationships that are more often than not intimately connected with one another rather than easily separable. Foucault's conception enables—indeed, requires—us to view the same action or relationship simultaneously in terms of power-over and in terms of power-to. In order to appreciate the gains of this kind of conception of power, let us consider an issue that has been the subject of much feminist debate: pornography. Some feminists—most notably MacKinnon and Dworkin[83]—have examined pornography solely through the lens of men's power over women. They have concluded that pornography upholds and reinforces (even creates?) male dominance and female submissiveness and, consequently, that it must be eradicated if women are to be free.[84] Other feminists have held precisely the opposite view of pornography.[85] They have criticized MacKinnon and Dworkin for ignoring or, worse, denying the power and agency that women experience through their sexuality; and to remedy this, they set out to analyze pornography through the lens of women's empowerment. Although these feminists do not deny that much pornography is created by and for men and that it presents women in a negative light, they maintain that pornography is a potentially liberating and empowering form of sexual expression for women. In some sense, each of these analyses of pornography finds what it is looking for: The former goes looking for confirmation of male domination over women, and the latter goes looking for possible sites of empowerment and resistance. Moreover, each is *able* to find what it is looking for only because pornography both constrains women and provides a possible site for their empowerment; furthermore, it constrains by enabling and enables by constraining. Only a conception of power that highlights the interplay between constraint—or the exercise of power-over—and enablement—or the exercise of power-to—such as Foucault's can give us the theoretical tools that allow us to understand such complex and variegated phenomena.[86]

To summarize: Foucault's microphysics of power resonates with feminists' insistence that the personal is political, his account of the impact of disciplinary power on the body has provided feminists with a useful model for investigating the particular ways in which power shapes women's bodies, and his investigation of the institutional sedimentation of power relations has inspired feminist analyses of the sedimentation of male power over women in the institutions of the welfare state. Most important, however, for my examination of Foucault, his theoretical framework for the study of power offers feminists a conception that highlights the interplay between constraint and enablement and thus allows us to move beyond the conceptual one-sidedness of the feminist accounts of power discussed in Chapter 1.

Limits to the Collaboration: Resistance, Agency, and Solidarity

Up to this point, I have defended Foucault's analysis of power from attack and argued that it provides crucial resources for a feminist conception of power. However, I do not wish to argue that feminists should adopt Foucault's account of power as it stands. A feminist conception of power that draws on Foucault's analysis of power will have to overcome several significant limitations. These limitations are the result of a set of lingering problems in Foucault's analysis of power: the problem of resistance, the problem of agency, and the problem of solidarity. I shall discuss each of these in turn.

The Problem of Resistance

Foucault repeatedly emphasizes that resistance is integral to any exercise of power; for instance, he writes, "Where there is power, there is resistance, and yet, or rather, consequently, this resistance is never in a position of exteriority in relation to power."[87] In other words, in his analysis, resistance and power are "coextensive."[88] There is a valuable insight to be gleaned from this account of the conceptual relationship between resistance and power: It teaches us to avoid thinking of resistance as a social relation that is fundamentally separate from and opposed to the exercise of power-over others. In this way, Foucault's account reminds us that resistance to domination can itself take the form of exercising power-over others. To take just one example of this phenomenon, consider the attempt in the late 1970s and early 1980s to pass the Equal Rights Amendment (ERA). In this case, feminist resistance to male domination took the form of placing the ERA on the ballot; in so doing, feminists were attempting to exercise power over those who did not agree with equal rights for women by codifying those rights in the Constitution, thus compelling all citizens to recognize and respect them.[89] In this instance, resis-

tance to power-over in turn took the form of an exercise of power-over;
indeed, Foucault's claim that power and resistance are coextensive can be
understood as offering valuable conceptual insight into this kind of situation.

Nevertheless, I maintain that Foucault falls short of providing an
analysis that can fully illuminate resistance to male domination. The
main reason for this is that he never offers a detailed account of resistance as an empirical phenomenon in any of his genealogical analyses.
The only social actors in those works are the dominating agents; there is
no discussion of the strategies employed by madmen, delinquents,
schoolchildren, perverts, or "hysterical" women to modify or contest the
disciplinary or bio-power exercised over them. *A fortiori*, Foucault never
made good on his profound aim of integrating his brilliant account of
power with an analysis of resistance. Instead, all he does is to posit the
conceptual necessity of resistance, which is unsatisfactory without an explanation of how resistance works, what makes it effective or ineffective,
what legitimates it, what motivates it, and so on.

One might object to this characterization of Foucault's work by claiming that, although he does not adequately address resistance in his genealogies of power, he does offer a thorough account of resistance in his
final works on the practices of the self in the Greek and Roman eras.[90]
Lois McNay makes such an argument; she claims that in Foucault's final
works, "individuals are no longer conceived as docile bodies in the grip
of an inexorable disciplinary power, but as self-determining agents who
are capable of challenging and resisting the structures of domination in
modern society."[91] In other words, McNay contends that Foucault's late
discussions of practices and techniques of the self provide the necessary
counterpoint to the relative lack of an empirical analysis of resistance in
his earlier work.

However, McNay's attempt to salvage Foucault's account of resistance
fails on two counts. First, her claim that, in his late works, Foucault offers
an account of "self-determining agents who are capable of challenging
and resisting the structures of domination in *modern society*"[92] conflates
two distinctly different and unrelated historical analyses. The last two
volumes of *The History of Sexuality* are not about modern society or its
structures of domination. On the contrary, they are about the techniques
of the self practiced in Hellenic Greece and classical Rome. Indeed, Foucault insists that we must be very careful not to hold up the Greeks as
role models for our own lives. Thus, McNay's characterization of the account of resistance in those works is highly problematic. Furthermore,
even if one were to accept that the account of the self developed in the
late Foucault could be separated from its historical context and used to
fill in the lacunae in the earlier genealogical works, the problem remains

that Foucault never offered much insight into how the account of the self in the late works might be integrated with the genealogies of power. Thus, a huge reconstructive project explaining just how the account of resistance in the late works might be integrated into the earlier discussion of power would have to be completed before we could agree with McNay that the late works fill in this gap in Foucault's earlier analysis.[93]

The problem of resistance represents a significant drawback for a feminist appropriation of Foucault's analysis of power to overcome. However, I suggest that it is primarily an empirical problem, not a conceptual one. The problem of resistance stems from the fact that Foucault never made good on his own conceptual analysis of the interplay between power and resistance. In other words, the resources available in Foucault's conception of power for understanding the relationship between domination and resistance are underdeveloped in his own genealogical analyses. Thus, it seems likely that the problem of resistance can potentially be overcome by simply paying more attention to the interplay between these two forces in a feminist analysis of power. I shall argue in Chapter 3 that Judith Butler's feminist genealogy of power develops the conceptual resources of Foucault's analysis more fully than Foucault himself did and, thus, that her work fills in this lacuna in his account of power.

The Problem of Agency

I argued above that the claim that Foucault eradicates the subject rests on a misreading of his methodological approach to the study of power. However, I acknowledged that Foucault's account of the subject is not wholly satisfactory—in particular, because it falls into what I shall call the paradox of agency. I have discussed in some detail Foucault's use of the term *subjection*, and his insistence that we are always subjects in both senses of that term. But this account of subjection leads Foucault into a paradox: On the one hand, if we are always subjects in the sense of being subjected to myriad power relations, then what seems to be implied is a rather deterministic account of human action that denies the possibility of human agency; on the other hand, if we are always subjects in the sense of having the capacity to act, then the implication seems to be a rather voluntaristic account of human action that denies the grip that power relations have on us. Simply combining these two radically different conceptions of human action into one concept implies that the best we can do is to learn to live with this paradox. But that doesn't seem to be a sustainable option. Furthermore, given the centrality of this paradox to Foucault's analysis, it is not surprising that commentators have tended to reject Foucault on the grounds that he falls down on one side or the other of the determinism/voluntarism divide.[94] What Foucault needs in order to be able to navigate this divide successfully is an account of what it is that mediates between the agency of subjects and the power that subjects them. Although Foucault himself never develops such an account, I shall argue in Chapter 3 that Judith Butler's reformulation and extension of Foucault's conception of power does; thus, Butler is able to resolve the Foucaultian paradox of agency.

The Problem of Solidarity

Foucault views power solely in strategic terms. Relations of power are, for him, the "means by which individuals try to conduct, to determine the behavior of others."[95] The assumption that power is fundamentally strategic commits Foucault to denying that power can grow out of an agreement among actors. In this vein, Foucault writes, "power is not a function of consent";[96] and "the relationship of power can be the result of a prior or permanent consent, but it is not by nature the manifestation of a consensus."[97] The problem with this strategic conception of power is that it commits Foucault to a wholesale rejection of any sort of under- standing of the power that is generated through reciprocal, collective so- cial action. This means that Foucault rules out the possibility of the kind of collective empowerment that makes possible feminist solidarity. As problematic as the concept of solidarity might be, the collective empow- erment of members of the women's movement has been an effective force for political change and has served as a crucial resource for individual women who are striving to resist male domination in their daily lives. Thus, a feminist conception of power ought to be able to shed light on solidarity. I shall argue in more detail in Chapter 3 that if this objective is to be achieved, we shall have to move beyond a Foucaultian approach to the study of power.

Conclusion

In conclusion, let me sum up the strengths and weaknesses of Foucault's highly provocative and original analysis of power. First, the strengths: Foucault's account displaces the conception of power that has tradition- ally been presupposed in political theory in a way that resonates with feminist attempts to expand the scope of political theory; his focus on the effects of power on the body has proved useful for feminist investiga- tions of the bodily effects of male dominance; his analysis of the sedimen- tation of power relations into institutions has inspired feminist genealo- gies of the ways in which the institutions of the welfare state enact and reinforce male dominance; and finally and most important, his analysis provides the crucial conceptual insight into the interplay between constraint and enablement that can allow us to move beyond the impasse reached by the feminist conceptions of power as domination and of power as empowerment discussed in Chapter 1.

Now, the weaknesses: As I discussed above, Foucault's analysis fails to make the kinds of conceptual and normative distinctions that a feminist analysis—indeed, any critical analysis —of power requires. I suggested that this problem can be corrected by supplying the conceptual and normative distinctions that Foucault fails to draw. However, this will have to be done in such a way that it won't be in blatant contradiction with the rest of Foucault's philosophical work. I believe it can be done by adopting normative concepts such as domination, justice, right, reciprocity, and so on, but understanding them as historically constructed and, thus, contingent and essentially contested concepts.[98]

The problem of resistance in Foucault's work can, I maintain, be overcome by providing the kind of rich genealogical analysis of resistance that he himself neglects to provide, thereby reaping the full benefit of his brilliant conceptual insight into the interplay between power and resistance. I shall argue in Chapter 3 that Judith Butler's Foucaultian-feminist genealogy of power makes good on this aim.

The problem of agency can likewise be overcome by providing an account of what mediates between individual agents and the network of power relations in which they are caught. Again, I shall argue in Chapter 3 that, despite a similar tendency to fall into the paradox of agency in her earlier work, Butler's more recent work is able to resolve this paradox by introducing the Derridean notion of citationality or iterability as that which mediates between the two poles of subjection.

The problem of solidarity, however, can be overcome only by rejecting Foucault's view that power is always strategic. Indeed, I would suggest that this view makes no sense even within the context of Foucault's own analyses of strategic deployments of power. After all, don't the guards in a prison have to work together to keep their position of power over the prisoners? Isn't their ability to exercise power over the prisoners in some sense a collective achievement? It seems to me that even strategic deployments of power sometimes require a prior moment of consensus or agreement; indeed, it is often the case that consensus or agreement is precisely that which allows strategic power to work efficiently. However, even if my contention is correct, the framework that Foucault develops for the study of power consistently denies this possibility; thus, in order to arrive at a conception that can illuminate collective empowerment and feminist solidarity, we will need to go beyond a Foucaultian framework. I shall discuss these issues in more detail when I consider Hannah Arendt's conception of power in Chapter 4.

In sum, Foucault's analysis provides an insight that is sorely lacking in many feminist discussions of power (although discussions inspired by Foucault—which I left out of my argument in Chapter 1—tend to be more successful in this regard): namely, the insight that constraint and enablement, domination and empowerment, are complexly intertwined. This insight allows us to move beyond some of the difficulties inherent in existing feminist discussions of power. Although there are some limitations to Foucault's account of power as it stands, many of these can be overcome from within a Foucaultian-feminist framework, as my discussion of Judith Butler's feminist genealogy of power in the following chapter aims to demonstrate.

Notes

1. The rejection of the equation of power with rule or law is something that Foucault shares with Hannah Arendt. I shall discuss this and other surprising similarities between Foucault and Arendt in more detail in Chapter 4.

2. Michel Foucault, *The History of Sexuality, Vol. 1: An Introduction*, trans. Robert Hurley (New York: Vintage, 1978), p. 85.

3. See, for example, Jürgen Habermas, *The Philosophical Discourse of Modernity*, trans. Frederick G. Lawrence (Cambridge, Mass.: MIT Press, 1987), ch. 10; Axel Honneth, *The Critique of Power: Reflective Stages in a Critical Social Theory*, trans. Kenneth Baynes (Cambridge, Mass.: MIT Press, 1991), chs. 5 and 6; Thomas McCarthy, "The Critique of Impure Reason: Foucault and the Frankfurt School," in McCarthy, *Ideals and Illusions: On Reconstruction and Deconstruction in Contemporary Critical Theory* (Cambridge, Mass.: MIT Press, 1991); and Michael Walzer, "The Politics of Michel Foucault," in David Couzens Hoy, ed., *Foucault: A Critical Reader* (Oxford: Blackwell, 1986).

4. For a sample of feminist discussions of Foucault, see Irene Diamond and Lee Quinby, eds., *Feminism and Foucault: Reflections on Resistance* (Boston: Northeastern University Press, 1988); Nancy Fraser, *Unruly Practices: Power, Discourse, and Gender in Contemporary Social Theory* (Minneapolis: University of Minnesota Press, 1989), chs. 1–3; Susan Hekman, ed., *Rereading the Canon: Feminist Interpretations of Foucault* (University Park: Pennsylvania State Press, 1996); Lois McNay, *Foucault and Feminism: Power, Gender, and the Self* (Boston: Northeastern University Press, 1992); and Jana Sawicki, *Disciplining Foucault: Feminism, Power, and the Body* (New York: Routledge, 1991).

5. I borrow this phrase from Linda Alcoff, "Feminist Politics and Foucault: The Limits to a Collaboration," in Arlene Dallery and Charles Scott, eds., *Crises in Continental Philosophy* (Albany: SUNY Press, 1991). Although I agree with Alcoff that there are limits to such a collaboration, I think that we disagree over exactly where those limits should be placed.

6. Michel Foucault, "Prison Talk," in Colin Gordon, ed., *Power/Knowledge: Selected Interviews and Other Writings, 1972–1977* (New York: Pantheon, 1980), pp. 53–54.

7. Michel Foucault, *Discipline and Punish: The Birth of the Prison*, trans. Alan Sheridan (New York: Vintage, 1979).

8. For a discussion of the "repressive hypothesis," see Foucault, *The History of Sexuality, Vol. 1*, pp. 15–49.

9. Foucault, "Two Lectures," in Gordon, ed., *Power/Knowledge*, p. 96.

10. Foucault, *Discipline and Punish*, p. 26.

11. Foucault, "Truth and Power," in Gordon, ed., *Power/Knowledge*, p. 119.

12. Foucault, *Discipline and Punish*, p. 23.

13. Ibid.

14. Ibid., p. 194.

15. Ibid., p. 277.

16. Foucault, *The History of Sexuality, Vol. 1*, p. 136.

17. Ibid.

18. Ibid., pp. 136–137.

19. Ibid., p. 12.

20. Ibid.

21. Judith Butler, "Sexual Inversions," in Domna Stanton, ed., *Discourses of Sexuality: From Aristotle to AIDS* (Ann Arbor: University of Michigan Press, 1992), p. 350.

22. See, for example, Foucault, "Two Lectures," p. 98; and Foucault, "Afterword: The Subject and Power," in Hubert Dreyfus and Paul Rabinow, *Michel Foucault: Beyond Structuralism and Hermeneutics* (Chicago: University of Chicago Press, 1982), p. 212.

23. Foucault, *Discipline and Punish*, p. 170.

24. I borrow this formulation from Fraser, "Foucault on Modern Power: Empirical Insights and Normative Confusions," in Fraser, *Unruly Practices*, p. 18.

25. Foucault, *The History of Sexuality, Vol. 1*, p. 60.

26. See Nancy Hartsock, "Foucault on Power: A Theory for Women?" in Linda Nicholson, ed., *Feminism/Postmodernism* (New York: Routledge, 1990), pp. 164–166; and Hartsock, "Community/Sexuality/Gender: Rethinking Power," in Nancy J. Hirschmann and Christine Di Stefano, eds., *Revisioning the Political: Feminist Reconstructions of Traditional Concepts in Western Political Theory* (Boulder: Westview Press, 1996), pp. 37–41.

27. Hartsock, "Community/Sexuality/Gender," p. 39.

28. Hartsock, "Foucault on Power," p. 166.

29. Ibid., pp. 166–167.

30. In this, Hartsock is far from alone. For other criticisms of Foucault's claim that the subject is an effect of power, see Linda Alcoff, "Feminist Politics and Foucault," p. 71; Jürgen Habermas, *The Philosophical Discourse of Modernity*, chs. 9 and 10; Axel Honneth, *The Critique of Power*; and Thomas McCarthy, "The Critique of Impure Reason."

31. Hartsock, "Foucault on Power," p. 163.

32. Hartsock, "Community/Sexuality/Gender," pp. 38–39. See also Edward Said, "Foucault and the Imagination of Power," in Hoy, ed., *Foucault: A Critical Reader*, pp. 151–152.

33. Michel Foucault, "Revolutionary Action: 'Until Now,'" in Donald F. Bouchard, ed., *Language, Counter-Memory, Practice* (Ithaca: Cornell University

Press, 1977), p. 220; cited in Hartsock, "Community/Sexuality/Gender," p. 39. Hartsock alters the quote in a significant way. The sentence actually reads: "Yet this knowledge has never been allowed to function [n'est jamais apparu] within official knowledge." I discuss this passage in more detail below.

34. Foucault, "Two Lectures," p. 81, pp. 85–86; cited in Hartsock, "Community/Sexuality/ Gender," p. 39.

35. Hartsock, "Community/Sexuality/Gender," p. 39.

36. For evidence that the displacement of the subject is a methodological and not a substantive move, see Foucault, "Two Lectures," pp. 97–98.

37. Foucault, "Revolutionary Action: 'Until Now,'" p. 222.

38. I develop this argument in much more detail in Amy Allen, "Foucault's Debt to Hegel," *Philosophy Today* 42:1 (1998): 71–78; and Amy Allen, "The Anti-Subjective Hypothesis: Michel Foucault and the Eradication of the Subject," paper presented at the annual meeting of the American Philosophical Association, Eastern Division, Philadelphia, December 1997.

39. Foucault, "Two Lectures," p. 82; emphasis added.

40. Foucault, "Revolutionary Action: 'Until Now,'" pp. 219–220.

41. Foucault, "Two Lectures," p. 83.

42. Ibid.

43. Ibid., p. 85.

44. See Nancy Hartsock, *Money, Sex, and Power: Toward a Feminist Historical Materialism* (Boston: Northeastern University Press, 1983), passim.

45. Hartsock, "Community/Sexuality/Gender," p. 39.

46. Ibid., p. 40.

47. Ibid.

48. Ibid.

49. See Foucault, *The History of Sexuality, Vol. 1*, p. 94.

50. Hartsock, "Community/Sexuality/Gender," p. 41.

51. Ibid.

52. Ibid.

53. Foucault, "Two Lectures," p. 100.

54. Ibid.

55. Ibid., p. 99

56. Foucault, *The History of Sexuality, Vol. 1*, p. 99.

57. It is true that Foucault did not leave us many detailed accounts of *how* this integration of local power relations into large, general power mechanisms takes place, but this does not mean that it is in principle impossible to provide such an account from within a Foucaultian analysis of power. Perhaps the best account he gives of this process is his discussion of "bio-power" (see Foucault, *The History of Sexuality, Vol. 1*, pp. 139–145). On this point, see also Fraser, "Foucault on Modern Power," pp. 24–25.

58. Michel Foucault, "The Ethic of Care for the Self as a Practice of Freedom," in James Bernauer and David Rasmussen, eds., *The Final Foucault* (Cambridge, Mass.: MIT Press, 1988), p. 3.

59. I am grateful to Richard Lynch for helping me to formulate this point.

60. Foucault, "Intellectuals and Power," in Bouchard, ed., *Language, Counter-Memory, Practice*, p. 213; emphasis added. For a similar claim, see "Two Lectures," p. 99.

61. Hartsock, "Community/Sexuality/Gender," p. 41.

62. Foucault, *The History of Sexuality, Vol. 1*, p. 94.

63. Foucault, "Two Lectures," pp. 100–101

64. Ibid., p. 101.

65. Fraser, "Foucault on Modern Power," p. 32.

66. Indeed, given the rather marginal place of this distinction in Foucault's work, one might object to my appeal to it in my response to Hartsock. However, even if it occurs only once, the way Foucault draws this distinction can be reformulated such that it is consistent with his general theoretical framework for analyzing power and with some of his earlier claims about power. For these reasons, my appeal to it does not seem to me to be problematic. For a similar appeal to Foucault's distinction between power and domination, see Sawicki, *Disciplining Foucault*, pp. 122–123, note 4.

67. Jana Sawicki explicitly argues for such an approach in response to Fraser's critique (see Sawicki, *Disciplining Foucault*, pp. 122–123, note 4). This also seems to be the approach that Fraser herself adopts in later writings that draw on Foucaultian genealogy but that don't shy away from making normative judgments. In this connection, see especially Nancy Fraser and Linda Gordon, "A Genealogy of 'Dependency': Tracing a Keyword of the U.S. Welfare State," *Signs* 19:2 (Winter 1994): 309–336; Fraser and Nicholson, "Social Criticism Without Philosophy," in Nicholson, ed., *Feminism/Postmodernism*; and Fraser, "False Antitheses: A Response to Seyla Benhabib and Judith Butler," in Seyla Benhabib et al., eds., *Feminist Contentions: A Philosophical Exchange* (New York: Routledge, 1995).

68. Foucault himself indicates that his work implies a deconstruction of gender (see "Revolutionary Action: 'Until Now,'" p. 222). For the best development of this line of thought in Foucault and other contemporary French theorists, see Judith Butler, *Gender Trouble: Feminism and the Subversion of Identity* (New York: Routledge, 1990).

69. Fraser, "Foucault on Modern Power," p. 18.

70. Nancy Hartsock's *Money, Sex, and Power* is an impressive and welcome exception to this trend. However, as should be clear from my discussion of Hartsock above, her view couldn't be further from Foucault's, or from my own, analysis of power.

71. Foucault, *Discipline and Punish*, p. 138.

72. Ibid., p. 228.

73. Sandra Bartky, "Foucault, Femininity, and the Modernization of Patriarchal Power," in Bartky, *Femininity and Domination* (New York: Routledge, 1990), p. 65.

74. See ibid., pp. 66–71.

75. For a similar example of this kind of analysis of the relationship between power and the female body, also inspired by Foucault, see Susan Bordo, "Anorexia Nervosa: Psychopathology as the Crystallization of Culture," in Bordo, *Unbearable Weight: Feminism, Western Culture, and the Body* (Berkeley: University of California Press, 1993).

76. Foucault, *Discipline and Punish*, pp. 202–203.

77. Bartky, "Foucault, Femininity, and the Modernization of Patriarchal Power," p. 80.

78. See the discussion of "complete and austere institutions" in Foucault, *Discipline and Punish*, pp. 231ff.

79. Fraser and Gordon, "A Genealogy of 'Dependency.'" Fraser and Gordon note that their approach diverges from Foucault's in two respects: First, they contextualize their genealogy in relation to "broad social-structural shifts"; second, they incorporate a normative dimension in their analysis (p. 311).

80. Ibid., pp. 310–311.

81. Fraser further develops this Foucault-inspired feminist analysis of the welfare state in "Women, Welfare and the Politics of Need Interpretation" and "Struggle Over Needs: Outline of a Socialist-Feminist Critical Theory of Late Capitalist Political Culture," both in *Unruly Practices*.

82. Foucault, "Afterword," p. 220.

83. See Andrea Dworkin, *Intercourse* (New York: Free Press, 1987), and *Pornography: Men Possessing Women* (New York: Plume, 1979); and Catharine MacKinnon, *Feminism Unmodified* (Cambridge, Mass.: Harvard University Press, 1987), *Only Words* (Cambridge, Mass.: Harvard University Press, 1993), and *Toward a Feminist Theory of the State* (Cambridge, Mass.: Harvard University Press, 1989).

84. It is important to note that the anti-pornography ordinance proposed by MacKinnon and Dworkin does not call for eradicating or banning pornography; instead, it makes pornography civilly actionable. However, given their analysis of pornography and the role that it plays in women's subordination, it seems clear that MacKinnon and Dworkin would be most happy if pornography were to disappear from the face of the earth, even though they stop short of attempting to make that happen legally.

85. See Ann Snitow et al., eds., *Powers of Desire: The Politics of Sexuality* (New York: Monthly Review Press, 1983); and Carole S. Vance, ed., *Pleasure and Danger: Exploring Female Sexuality* (New York: Routledge, 1990).

86. Obviously, this issue is more complex than the present discussion indicates; I plan to analyze the conceptions of power implicit in the feminist pornography debate in more detail in a future paper.

87. Foucault, *The History of Sexuality, Vol. 1*, p. 95.

88. Michel Foucault, "Power and Sex," in Lawrence D. Kritzman, ed., *Michel Foucault: Politics, Philosophy, Culture* (New York: Routledge, 1988), p. 122.

89. I am indebted to Jane Mansbridge for this example. For an excellent discussion of power relations with respect to the ERA, see Mansbridge, *Why We Lost the ERA* (Chicago: University of Chicago Press, 1986).

90. See Michel Foucault, *The Use of Pleasure, Volume Two of the History of Sexuality*, trans. Robert Hurley (New York: Vintage, 1985), and *The Care of the Self: Volume Three of the History of Sexuality*, trans. Robert Hurley (New York: Vintage, 1986).

91. McNay, *Foucault and Feminism*, p. 4.

92. Ibid.; emphasis added.

93. Indeed, McNay's interpretation of Foucault's late work makes it difficult to see how such an integration could be possible, insofar as, in her view, "Foucault's

final work on the self represents a significant shift from the theoretical concerns of his earlier work" (see McNay, *Foucault and Feminism*, p. 4).

94. To be sure, most critics accuse him of falling into the trap of determinism; hence, they seek to label him as a structuralist or functionalist. Their doing so is perhaps related to the fact that most critics focus on Foucault's early- and middle-period works to the exclusion of the last two volumes of *The History of Sexuality*, in which Foucault focuses on the agency side of this split. Thomas McCarthy does a nice job of diagnosing the parallel tendencies to collapse into determinism in the early and middle work and into voluntarism in the late work (see McCarthy, "The Critique of Impure Reason," p. 70).

95. Foucault, "Ethic of Care for the Self," p. 18.

96. Foucault, "Afterword," pp. 219–220.

97. Ibid., p. 220.

98. Cf. Fraser, "Struggle over Needs," in Fraser, *Unruly Practices*, p. 187; Fraser and Nicholson, "Social Criticism Without Philosophy"; and Sawicki, *Disciplining Foucault*, p. 123.

3

Power Trouble:
Judith Butler's Feminist
Genealogy of Power

Judith Butler's theory of the performativity of gender has caused quite a
stir in feminist circles. Butler has been both idolized and vilified for her
claim that sex, no less than gender, is not biologically or naturally based
but is discursively constructed and performatively produced and reproduced. But though the implications of the theory of performativity for
the feminist analysis of sex/gender have been explored in some detail, its
implications for a feminist analysis of power have not. Perhaps this is because it is assumed that Butler simply adopts without modification a
Foucaultian analysis of power; thus, it is assumed that feminist discussions of Foucault's account of power apply, *mutatis mutandis*, to Butler as
well. Indeed, there is some plausibility to this view, especially if one focuses one's attention on Butler's groundbreaking early work, *Gender
Trouble*.[1] In that book, Butler more or less straightforwardly adopts a Foucaultian analysis of power and, along with it, all of the insights and ob-
fuscations such an analysis invites. However, in her more recent reformulations of the theory of performativity, Butler moves beyond Foucault's
analysis of power by providing one of the crucial ingredients that his
analysis lacked: an account of what it is that mediates between the two
poles of subjection, between individual subjects and the oppressive
sex/gender norms to which they are subjected. I shall argue that, by providing this missing ingredient, Butler has been able to move beyond the
Foucaultian paradox of agency and to provide an account of power that
succeeds to some extent in theorizing simultaneously *both* the features of
cultural domination in contemporary societies *and* the possibilities of resistance to and subversion of such domination. Thus, despite some significant limitations to the account of power that is implicit in the theory

of performativity, this account proves to be quite fruitful for the development of a feminist conception of power.

I begin in the first section by laying out the conception of power implicit in *Gender Trouble*, Butler's early formulation of the theory of performativity. I demonstrate the ways in which, in that work, Butler adopts a Foucaultian framework and, hence, inherits the Foucaultian problem diagnosed in Chapter 2: the paradox of agency. As a result of this inheritance, *Gender Trouble* founders on the traditional philosophical cleavage between determinism and voluntarism. After laying out this troubling implication of her early formulation of performativity, I go on in the second section to examine Butler's recent reformulations—in her books *Bodies That Matter: On the Discursive Limits of "Sex"*[2] and *Excitable Speech: A Politics of the Performative*,[3] and in her contribution to *Feminist Contentions: A Philosophical Exchange*[4]—which attempt to overcome this problem by appealing to the Derridean notion of citationality or iterability. I maintain that this notion allows Butler to make the crucial link between sexed individuals and the culturally hegemonic norms that govern their production that was missing in her early formulation. Citationality thus solves one of the problems plaguing the theory of performativity and allows Butler to begin to move feminist discussions of power beyond their current impasse. Despite its solution of the Foucaultian problem of agency, however, significant problems remain. I conclude by discussing three limitations to Butler's analysis that must be overcome before her account can be truly productive for a feminist critical theory of power.

Performativity: Take One

Butler's first formulation of performativity theory, *Gender Trouble*, starts with a reflection on the category of "women." She criticizes various approaches to feminism that turn on unproblematized notions of identity and identity politics. Such approaches ignore both the Foucaultian insight that all identities are effects of productive/repressive power regimes, and the objection, raised by many feminists of color, that the category of "women" has traditionally excluded everyone except white, middle-class, academic women. Instead of assuming from the outset that there must be a universal basis for feminism, Butler claims that "feminist critique ought also to understand how the category of 'women,' the subject of feminism, is produced and restrained by the very structures of power through which emancipation is sought."[5] In other words, feminist critique requires a *"feminist genealogy* of the category of women."[6]

Gender Trouble offers just such a genealogy, and it yields two potentially surprising results. First, it is among the first works in feminist theory to challenge the sex/gender distinction. Throughout the 1970s and 1980s, feminists, with few exceptions,[7] had accepted the distinction between "sex"—the natural, physical differences between biological males and females—and "gender"—the socially and culturally constructed patterns of femininity and masculinity that are tied to biological sex and reified into the categories of "men" and "women." Feminist critique had restricted itself to an assault on gender and the unjust system of domination that comes along with it; sex, on the other hand, was considered to be biologically based, natural, and, therefore, out of the bounds of critique. Against this received wisdom, Butler argues that "gender is not to culture as sex is to nature; gender is also the discursive/cultural means by which 'sexed nature' or 'a natural sex' is produced and established as 'prediscursive,' prior to culture, a politically neutral surface *on which* culture acts."[8] The first result of the feminist genealogy of "women," then, is the contention that sex is every bit as culturally produced as gender; far from being natural, sex has been culturally constructed and falsely naturalized.

The second result is the theory of performativity itself. Butler contends that "gender" is not a noun with a fixed set of attributes. On the contrary,

> gender proves to be performative—that is, constituting the identity it is purported to be. In this sense, gender is always a doing, though not a doing by a subject who might be said to preexist the deed. . . . [Paraphrasing Nietzsche] there is no gender identity behind the expressions of gender; that identity is performatively constituted by the very "expressions" that are said to be its results.[9]

If gender is continually enacted and performed, then, according to Butler, it is possible for individuals to alter their performances in ways that might subvert the heterosexist norms that govern its very production. Everything turns, in other words, on how we perform our gender (for, make no mistake about it, we are all compelled to perform in one way or another): If I perform the role of "woman" timidly and faithfully, my performance is likely to uphold heterosexist domination; if, on the other hand, I perform flamboyantly, irreverently, and parodically, my performance subverts such domination.

In this way, Butler attempts to account for the interrelation between oppressive gender norms and the possibilities for resistance to such norms that are opened up by the performance of gender. Moreover, she denies that such subversion is the result either of a humanist assertion of the will or of an existentialist authentically free choice. She writes: "If power is not reduced to volition, . . . and the classical liberal and existential model of freedom is refused, then power relations can be understood, as I think they ought to be, as constraining and constituting the very possibilities of volition. Hence, power can neither be withdrawn nor refused, but only redeployed."[10]

However, it is at this point that the traditional philosophical distinction between determinism and voluntarism begins to cause Butler trouble. As the passage just cited makes clear, her claim that power can be neither withdrawn nor refused is cast as an explicit attempt to avoid voluntarism. However, this, in turn, raises the question of how it is possible that the relations of power with which feminism contends can ever be changed; that is to say, it raises the question of how Butler's denial of voluntarism can avoid falling into determinism. Butler insists that her analysis avoids determinism because it contains a viable conception of agency: Agency, in Butler's view, consists in the ability to introduce a potentially subversive variation on the compulsory repetition of normatively prescribed acts. Thus, according to Butler, the theory of performativity avoids determinism because it views individuals as capable of performing heterosexist norms in such a way as to make them into a "site of parodic contest and display that robs compulsory heterosexuality of its claims to naturalness and originality."[11] Yet it is precisely this claim that raises the specter of voluntarism once again. Her idea that we may accomplish a subversion of compulsory heterosexuality by performing parodically rather than faithfully—for example, by dressing up in drag—implies that we are capable of consciously and willfully deciding how to enact our gender. The question is, How, in light of the complex cultural and social norms and power relations that Butler has analyzed, is such a decision possible? And, insofar as our identity is constituted in and through our performance, *who* could be making such a decision? Furthermore, how can we be sure that such parodic performances are effective? What guarantees that such performances will subvert, rather than leave untouched or, worse, unwittingly reinforce, the gender norms that they attack?

The result of this unresolved tension between determinism and voluntarism is that Butler's early formulation of the theory of gender performativity is paradoxically vulnerable to critique from completely opposite directions. Thus, those critics who have interpreted the text as coming down on the side of determinism accuse the theory of performativity of being unable to make sense of resistance to oppressive gender norms. This accusation often stems from a critique of Butler's relentless deconstruction of identity. Butler's call for the subversion of identity is rooted in her belief that *all* forms of identity are functions of repressive, exclusionary, binary oppositions that strive to conceal their own dominance by presenting historically, socially, and culturally constructed identity categories as natural and, thus, necessary. Butler's argument is designed to highlight the falsely naturalized and, thus, contingent character of these identity categories, which in turn is supposed to explain how resistance to and subversion of such categories is possible. However, Allison Weir claims that, by assuming that *all* forms of identity are inherently repressive and exclusionary, "Butler subverts her own call for a subversion of identity by rendering identity so omnipotent and intransigent that the subversion becomes impossible."[12] In order to explain how resistance and subversion of repressive identity categories are possible, Weir claims that Butler needs to differentiate between positive and negative conceptions of identity and to retain some sort of positive conception that could serve as the basis for social struggle.

Similarly, Seyla Benhabib argues that Butler's relentless deconstruction of the identity of the self leads the theory of performativity into the trap of determinism. Referring to Butler's embrace of Nietzsche's farewell to "the doer behind the deed,"[13] Benhabib asks,

> If this view of the self is adopted, is there any possibility of changing the "expressions" which constitute us? If we are no more than the sum total of the gendered expressions we perform, is there ever any chance to stop the performance for a while, to pull the curtain down, and let it rise only if one can have a say in the production of the play itself? Isn't this what the struggle over gender is all about?[14]

On the basis of this argument, Benhabib reaches the strong conclusion that the theory of performativity—along with all other postmodern theories that presuppose such a strong deconstruction of the subject—is not just an inadequate realization of feminist principles but is incompatible with the very goals of feminism itself.

However, if *Gender Trouble* was open to the charge that it theoretically undermined the very subversion and resistance it attempted to cultivate, it was no less open to the charge that it made subversion and resistance seem altogether too easy. Whereas Weir and Benhabib worry that Butler's theory implies a cultural determinism, Susan Bordo sees exactly the opposite tendency at work: Butler's focus on highly abstract, linguistic forms of cultural signification coupled with her postmodern celebration of subversion and contestation give the impression that resistance to gender oppression is simply a matter of making up one's mind to parody existing gender norms (for instance, by dressing up in drag). Bordo maintains that "this is ingenious and exciting, and it sounds right—in theory. And so long as we regard the body in drag as an abstract, unsituated linguistic structure, as pure text, we may be convinced by Butler's claim that the gender system is continually being playfully destabilized and subverted from within."[15] However, once we regard the body as the complex function not just of discourse but also of particular social and historical practices and contexts (as Bordo argues persuasively that we should), then it becomes clear that subversion and resistance are neither as simple nor as successful as Butler assumes them to be. A consideration of social and historical context muddies these waters considerably. For instance, Bordo notes, "Drag star Chili Pepper, speaking on the 'Donahue' show, said without irony that he felt drag queens could help teach women how to be 'real women.' . . . How culturally subversive can these forms be if they are so readily interpreted as proof of the foundational nature of gender, the essential reality of the 'binary frame'?"[16] Bordo concludes that Butler's inattention to social, historical and contextual factors leads her to be overly optimistic about the possibilities for subversion and resistance: "Butler's texts become signifiers without context, and her analysis begins to exhibit . . . a characteristically postmodern inclination to emphasize and celebrate resistance, the creative agency of individuals, and the instabilities of current power-relations rather than their recuperative tendencies."[17]

Whereas Benhabib and Weir link up Butler's determinism with her acceptance of the postmodern critique of the subject and of identity, Bordo links up her peculiar linguistic voluntarism with her embrace of the oppositional spirit of postmodernism. It is my contention that Butler's early formulation of the theory of performativity is open to these opposed— even contradictory—interpretations and criticisms because it remains caught in the Foucaultian paradox of agency. In her early work, Butler accepts without substantial modification Foucault's account of subjection; indeed, it is the jumping-off point for her argument. Thus, she writes at the opening of *Gender Trouble,*

> Foucault points out that juridical systems of power *produce* the subjects they subsequently come to represent. Juridical notions of power appear to regulate political life in purely negative terms. . . . But the subjects regulated by such structures are, by virtue of being subjected to them, formed, defined, and reproduced in accordance with the requirements of those structures.[18]

However, by accepting Foucault's account of subjection, Butler also takes on the Foucaultian paradox of agency. As I argued in Chapter 2, Foucault's account of subjection attempts to bring together two radically different conceptions of human subjectivity into one concept without providing an account of what it is that mediates between the agency of subjects and the power that subjects them. The Foucaultian conception of subjection thus presents us with an unsustainable paradox. Insofar as the theory of performativity as it is presented in *Gender Trouble* rests on this conception, it, too, presents such a paradox.[19] As a result, if we accept Butler's claim that the compulsory norms of heterosexist domination actually produce individual sexed and gendered agents, then her account of the agency of sexed and gendered individuals becomes hard to swallow, and if we accept her claims about the subversion and resistance of individual agents, then her analysis of heterosexist domination seems too thin. The upshot of this problem is that readers of *Gender Trouble* are left with the paradoxical feeling that resistance is either completely impossible or too easy. The early formulation of gender performativity is thus unsuccessful at conceptualizing the interplay between heterosexist domination and the possibilities for resisting such domination. What Butler needs, but doesn't yet have in this early work, is an account of that which mediates between the compulsory norms of heterosexist domination and the sexed/gendered individuals who perform them. This is what she finds in the Derridean notion of citationality or iterability.

Performativity: Take Two

In the preface to *Bodies That Matter*, Butler discusses the voluntarism/determinism problem raised by her first formulation of the theory of performativity. Claiming that gender is performative, she notes, "could mean that I thought that one woke in the morning, perused the closet or some more open space for the gender of choice, donned that gender for the day, and then restored the garment to its place at night."[20] If the theory of performativity is interpreted in this way, then it seems that one willfully chooses one's gender; but this means that Butler's view relies upon a voluntaristic—indeed, humanist—notion of choice and agency that is antithetical to the theory's constructivist aims. On the other hand, Butler asks, if the performance of gender is not the result of a choice, then "how are we to understand the constitutive and compelling status of gender norms without falling into the trap of cultural determinism?"[21] Her later formulations of the theory of performativity attempt to rethink this worrisome implication of *Gender Trouble*.[22]

In her contribution to *Feminist Contentions*—an exchange among Seyla Benhabib, Butler, Drucilla Cornell, and Nancy Fraser—Butler begins to deal with this problem by clarifying what she means by performativity. She indicates that her understanding of performativity is not derived from a behaviorist model according to which, as Benhabib put it in the passage quoted above, "we are no more than the sum total of the gendered expressions we perform."[23] Instead, she bases her use of the term "performativity" on J. L. Austin's account of performative utterances. In Austin's speech act theory, a performative is an utterance that enacts or produces that which it names (e.g., "I now pronounce you husband and wife"). However, Butler views speech act theory as problematic because it tends to presume a humanist subject who has the authority to call certain phenomena into being through his or her utterance (e.g., the priest, minister, or justice of the peace who is vested with the power to marry heterosexual couples). To avoid this implication, Butler draws on Derrida's reformulation of the performative. In this reformulation, the performative utterance is a derivative citation rather than a founding act by an originating subject. Derrida suggests that performatives are actually citations by asking, "Could a performative utterance succeed if its formulation did not repeat a 'coded' or iterable utterance, or in other words, if the formula I pronounce in order to open a meeting, launch a ship or a marriage were not identifiable as *conforming* with an iterable model, if it were not then identifiable in some way as a 'citation'?"[24]

In *Bodies That Matter*, Butler adopts this Derridean understanding of performativity as citationality and recasts the performativity of gender accordingly. In this reformulated view, the hegemonic cultural definitions that govern the production of sexuality (and, thus, of sexed bodies) cannot reproduce and sustain themselves; rather, they must be cited or reiterated by individuals in order to be reproduced and sustained. Thus, performativity must be understood as "a process of iterability, a regularized and constrained repetition of norms."[25] Moreover, Butler claims that it is the necessity of this reiteration that opens up the space for citations or reiterations that subvert precisely those norms that they are supposed to reinforce. As Butler puts it, a citation of a norm is not just an interpretation of that norm, it is also "an occasion to expose the norm itself as a privileged interpretation."[26] It is crucial to note that, in this later formulation of performativity theory, a citation is only an *occasion* to subvert a norm; it is no *guarantee* that the norm will be subverted. Although this point was far from clear in her earlier formulation, Butler now acknowledges that some citations will unwittingly reproduce the very norms that they seek to subvert. For instance, in her analysis of the film *Paris Is Burning*,[27] Butler emphasizes that drag is not necessarily subversive, and that it may very well reinforce and uphold the heterosexist norms that it parodies.[28] By underscoring this point, Butler responds to the objection—raised, for example, by Bordo and by Fraser[29]—that the theory of performativity assumes but fails to explain why resignification is necessarily subversive rather than reactionary or simply ineffectual. Butler now insists that resignification isn't necessarily subversive; the fact that norms must be cited in order for them to remain in force does not mean that citationality is a sufficient condition for subversion, only that it is a necessary one.

Once the idea of citationality is introduced, it becomes clear that performativity "is not a singular 'act' or event, but . . . a ritual reiterated under and through constraint."[30] It is the introduction of the concept of citationality or iterability and the claim that performativity is not an "act" that enables Butler to finesse the divide between determinism and voluntarism and to move beyond the Foucaultian paradox of agency. Gender performance is not an act by a voluntarist subject who simply chooses which sex or gender to be; rather, it is a compelled reiteration of norms that constructs individuals as sexed and gendered. In a more recent work, Butler makes it clear that this reiteration is compelled via the force of interpellation; thus, she writes, "the performative is not a singular act by an already established subject, but one of the powerful and insidious ways in which subjects are called into being from diffuse social quarters, inaugurated into sociality by a variety of diffuse and powerful interpellations."[31] However, the very fact that it is *necessary* for norms to be reiterated or cited by individuals in order for them to maintain their efficacy indicates that we are never completely determined by them. According to Butler, gender is an assignment, but "it is an assignment which is never quite carried out according to expectation, whose addressee never quite inhabits the ideal s/he is compelled to approximate."[32] In other words, gender norms are, in principle, unrealizable; they "are continually haunted by their own inefficacy; hence, the anxiously repeated effort to install and augment their jurisdiction."[33] If we were completely determined by gender norms, there would be no need for us to continually cite and reiterate them; that we are continually compelled to do so gives us good reason for thinking that we are not so determined.

The introduction of citationality thus allows Butler to think through the paradox of subjection that she inherits from Foucault and that causes the theory of performativity trouble in *Gender Trouble*. To be sure, Butler still accepts the basic structure of Foucault's analysis of subjection. As she writes in the opening of *The Psychic Life of Power*, "As a form of power, subjection is paradoxical. To be dominated by a power external to oneself is a familiar and agonizing form power takes. To find, however, that what 'one' is, one's very formation as a subject, is in some sense dependent upon that very power is quite another."[34] That is, Butler continues to maintain that one is both *subject to* the power of the heterosexist cultural norms that constrain and compel one's performance of gender and simultaneously enabled to take up the position of *a subject* in and through them. However, although Butler's second formulation of performativity theory accepts Foucault's analysis of subjection as a point of departure, it goes beyond Foucault to claim that the constitution of sex as an effect of such regulatory power is both "reiterated and reiterable."[35] As a result, Butler's reformulated theory of performativity provides what was missing both in Foucault's analysis of power and in her own early work: an account of citationality as that which mediates between regulatory power and the individual subjects that are both produced and controlled, enabled and constrained by it. The result is a mediated account of the subject that enables Butler to navigate the divide between deterministic norms and voluntaristic acts.

By incorporating the notion of citationality or iterability into her account of performativity, Butler is thus able to move beyond the Foucaultian paradox of agency and to negotiate the complex dialectical interplay between the domination enforced by heterosexist norms and individual refusal of, resistance to, or subversion of those norms. As a result, Butler's work makes a crucial contribution to a critical theory of power aimed at illuminating women's subordination that is attempting to move beyond the conceptions of power considered in Chapter 1.

The theoretical gains that Butler's theory of performativity offers to a feminist critical theory of power can be best understood if we consider how Butler has put this theory to work in the illumination of specific problems or issues. In *Excitable Speech*, Butler applies her theory of performativity to several of the most pressing political questions of our day: racist hate speech, pornography, and the discourse about gays in the military. In order to see precisely how Butler's conception of power benefits a feminist critical theory of power, I shall briefly examine her own application of it to the feminist debate over pornography.

Butler frames her discussion as an evaluation of Catharine MacKinnon's trenchant feminist critique of pornography. According to Butler, MacKinnon's view is overly deterministic; MacKinnon believes that pornography seamlessly constitutes women's reality, inexorably constructing women as sexually subordinate.[36] In this way, Butler indicates that she might agree with my characterization of MacKinnon in Chapter 1 as one of a group of feminists who have focused on domination to the exclusion of agency and resistance and, thus, have rendered their theories blind to the power that women are able to exercise. The problem with this sort of view, according to Butler, is that it grants too much power to pornography and not enough to women; she insists that the power evinced by pornography is "more frail and less deterministic" than MacKinnon makes it out to be.[37] Butler's account of the power relations at work in pornography, by contrast, draws on her theorization of the complex dialectical interplay between domination and resistance. According to Butler, pornography offers a depiction of a set of gender norms that individuals are compelled to cite; however, given Butler's understanding of performativity, these norms are in principle unrealizable and the very fact that they have to be cited in order to remain in force opens up a space for their subversion. Thus, Butler writes,

> pornography neither represents nor constitutes what women are, but offers an allegory of masculine willfulness and feminine submission (although these are clearly not its only themes), one which repeatedly and anxiously

rehearses its own *un*realizability. . . . Indeed, one might suggest that pornography is the text of gender's unreality, the impossible norms by which it is compelled, and in the face of which it continually fails.[38]

Furthermore, because MacKinnon relies on too simplistic a notion of power, her solution to the problem posed by pornography—making pornography open to civil litigation—is too easy. According to Butler, "Our work is more difficult, for what pornography delivers is what it recites and exaggerates from the resources of compensatory gender norms, a text of insistent and faulty imaginary relations that will not disappear with the abolition of the offending text, the text that remains for feminist criticism relentlessly to read."[39] Since Butler's conception of power emphasizes the role that women play in citing and potentially subverting the gender norms that they are compelled to repeat, her analysis of pornography avoids the problem of portraying women as victims, while still taking seriously the way that pornography figures in women's subordination insofar as it presents the cultural norms of masculine dominance and feminine submissiveness that individuals are compelled to cite.

A detailed discussion and evaluation of this contribution to the feminist pornography debate would require more time and space than are available here. However, such a detailed discussion is unnecessary for our purposes. The brief account that I have sketched of Butler's application of performativity theory to an analysis of pornography can provide enough of a sense of the gains afforded by such a theory. Since the theory of performativity provides a complicated account of the interplay between individuals and socially and culturally hegemonic power structures, when it is applied to a specific issue such as pornography, the result is an analysis that simultaneously accounts for both the cultural domination that is depicted in and reinforced by pornography and the possibilities of resistance to and subversion of such domination.

Limitations to Performativity

However, if the theory of performativity offers gains to a feminist critical theory of power, it incurs some losses as well. Three of these losses are significant enough that they make me hesitant to claim that Butler offers a completely successful feminist analysis of power. First, in *Bodies That Matter*, as elsewhere, Butler is uncomfortable with claiming that there is a normative dimension to her analysis. She writes, "If there is a 'normative' dimension to this work, it consists precisely in assisting a radical resignification of the symbolic domain . . . to expand the very meaning of what counts as a valued and valuable body in the world."[40] However, it is not clear that the call for resignification *is* a normative demand. The fact that Butler places the word *normative* in quotation marks makes it clear that she is uncomfortable with labeling it in this way. Given her equation of normativity per se with exclusion, there is good reason for this discomfort; for instance, in "Contingent Foundations," she writes, "Identity categories are never merely descriptive, but always normative, *and as such, exclusionary.*"[41] Nancy Fraser has aptly described the implications of this equation: "Deconstructive critique—critique that dereifies or unfreezes identity—is the privileged mode of feminist theorizing, whereas normative, reconstructive critique is normalizing and oppressive."[42]

Further, even if we grant for the moment that the call for a resignification *is* a normative demand, it is not the only nor even the most significant normative dimension of Butler's theory of performativity. The call for resignification relies on a prior normative claim that is implicit in Butler's analysis—namely, the claim that gender and sex *ought* to be subverted because they are unnatural cultural constructs that are falsely presented as natural. Butler claims that when a performance succeeds in being subversive it does so insofar as it *"disputes heterosexuality's claim on naturalness."*[43] If oppressive sex/gender norms function by taking on a mask of naturalness, then subverting such norms turns on exposing them as unnatural and falsely naturalized, on what Butler calls a "denaturalization of sex."[44] But why should we resignify these norms? Why expose them as unnatural? Why denaturalize sex? The answer has to be that unnatural constructs that parade as natural are, in some sense, bad and deserve to be subverted.

My point is not that Butler's work lacks the kind of normative foundation that grounds critique but, rather, that her theory of performativity already fundamentally relies on such a not-so-contingent foundation, whether Butler acknowledges this or not. As Nancy Fraser puts it, "Butler has explicitly renounced the moral-theoretical resources necessary to account for her own implicit normative judgments."[45] As a result of this renunciation, we aren't really left with a good reason for agreeing with her that sex/gender norms should be resisted and resignified because they have been falsely naturalized. Without a specific argument to the contrary, there seems to be no reason to agree with Butler that such unnatural constructs are, in themselves, objectionable. What is so bad about the unnatural? I would think that, at most, unnatural constructs would be normatively neutral, rather than normatively problematic. One might respond that what is wrong with these constructs is not that they are unnatural but that they are *falsely* naturalized. Then, one could say that by exposing sex and gender norms as unnatural, one tells the truth about them, shows them for what they *really* are. Indeed, at times it sounds as if Butler is making precisely this claim. However, this claim contradicts the

Foucaultian insight—which Butler embraces—that the compulsion to tell the truth about sex is but another deployment of power. Furthermore, the desire to tell the truth about sex presupposes precisely the kind of representationalist view of language that Butler claims to be moving beyond.[46] As a result of these performative contradictions (if you'll pardon the phrase), an appeal to the truth about the unnaturalness of sex does not seem to me to be an option that is open to Butler. I think that a better option is for Butler to admit without so much hesitation that she needs some normative concepts (feminist theory cannot get along without them), and to spend some time and energy defending the ones that are already lurking in her text.

The second hesitation stems from what I shall call Butler's linguistic monism. Rather than analyzing the power relations that serve to reinforce or subvert heterosexist gender norms in terms of both discursive and nondiscursive, linguistic and bodily practices, Butler insists upon reading all nondiscursive, bodily practices—indeed, bodies themselves—as discursive productions, as texts. Just as *Gender Trouble* aimed to show that the category of women was an effect of discursive production, *Bodies That Matter* aims to show that the compulsory norms of sex and gender "work . . . to constitute the materiality of bodies and, more specifically, to materialize the body's sex, to materialize sexual difference."[47] Thus, the body itself is not only an effect of power, it is "power's most productive effect."[48] In Butler's view, there may be a body outside of or beyond discourse, but any attempt to invoke such a pre- or extra-discursive body ignores the ways in which that invocation is itself discursive and, moreover, constitutive of the body as discursive. Thus, Butler writes, "to 'refer' naively . . . to such an extra-discursive object will always require the prior delimitation of the extra-discursive. And insofar as the extra-discursive is delimited, *it is formed by the very discourse from which it seeks to free itself.*"[49] This is what Butler means when she says that her concern is not with the matter of the body but with the way that "bodies come to matter at all"[50]—that is, with the discursive conditions of matter's possibility.

In a review of *Bodies That Matter* published in *Signs*, Jacqueline Zita is sharply critical of the way in which Butler's discursive account underplays or even ignores the facticity of the body. Zita calls for an alternative feminist theory of the body that would refuse the postmodern tendency to reduce the body to a discursive production. Such a theory, Zita suggests, might

> begin with the Mexican workers who have lost hands and arms in the meat-packing factories in my city, with where I will put my body to protect native fishing rights or keep the doors for abortion clinics open, or where I will station my body to protect gender outlaws in the ladies' room or, for that matter,

in the classroom. Certainly, one could take me aside to point out that even here the body has to be read and interpreted as a discursive effect, . . . but bodies also fall dead, bleed, vomit, break, and fall to pieces. The question of who dies is not an unintelligible question. . . . Is death also a discursive effect?[51]

In her defense, Butler claims that her view does not commit her to linguistic monism; thus, anticipating critiques of the sort that Zita makes, she maintains that she has never claimed that there is no outside to that which is discursively constructed, and she insists that "the point has never been that 'everything is discursively constructed.'"[52] To make such claims, Butler notes, would be to construe constructivism too simplistically and to concede an iron-clad determinism. Butler insists that she avoids this simplistic and deterministic version of constructivism because, for her, to claim that discourse is constitutive of bodies is "not to claim that it originates, causes, or exhaustively composes that which it concedes; rather, it is to claim that there is no reference to a pure body which is not at the same time a further formation of that body."[53] Thus, she invokes the limits of discourse as a defense against the claim that she writes the body out of existence; discourse constructs the body, but that construction is never seamless, monolithic, or even entirely successful; the body always exceeds its discursive construction.

Butler's analysis of the ways that linguistic norms produce ideals that are in principle impossible for individuals to realize, and of the ways that the body exceeds the discursive construction of materiality, is carried even further in her more recent book, *Excitable Speech*. There, she criticizes as naive the assumption that speech is always efficacious. The monolithic efficacy of speech is presupposed in the "don't ask, don't tell" policy adopted by the U.S. military toward gay and lesbian soldiers. This policy ascribes what Butler calls a "magical efficacy to words" insofar as "the declaration that one is a homosexual is understood to communicate something of homosexuality and, hence, to be a homosexual act of some kind."[54] Over and against this naive view of the magical efficacy of language, Butler suggests that "the term [*homosexuality*] cannot fully or exhaustively perform its referent [i.e., constitute the very sexuality to which it refers], *that no term can*, and that 'it's a good thing, too.'"[55] According to Butler, this is a good thing because, as I discussed above, it is precisely the failure of language to fully constitute its referent that opens up the space for resistance and subversion.

But this seems to me to beg an important question. In Butler's theory of performativity, discourse is undeniably powerful: After all, Butler argues persuasively that the body, the subject, the agent, woman, man, black, white, gay, lesbian, and straight are all discursively produced, maintained, and regulated. How, then, can discourse be all-powerful and yet so inherently flawed and ineffective? Butler's answer to this question is that discourse *must* be flawed and ineffective, otherwise individuals wouldn't have to continually cite the linguistic norms that govern the production of sexuality in order for them to remain in force. At some level, this response makes sense. But it fails to be completely satisfying because it does not answer the question of why such norms are ineffective. Why, to put it somewhat crudely, are these linguistic norms powerful enough to constitute us but not powerful enough to constitute us in any way that they please?

To answer this question satisfactorily, I think one has to move away from Butler and back to Foucault, or, perhaps, to push Butler back toward her Foucaultian roots. Butler's answer seems to be that the inefficacy of linguistic norms is just part of the paradoxical functioning of power. However, it strikes me as much more illuminating to answer this question in Foucaultian terms, to say that such linguistic norms are haunted by their own inefficacy because they do not work alone—they have to contend with various bodily, nondiscursive practices that may work alongside and reinforce them, or may work at cross-purposes with and subvert them. But this would be to accept that there are aspects of social and cultural life and of who we are as social and cultural actors that cannot be explained solely in terms of discourse. My point here is not that Butler's conception of power necessarily collapses into determinism but, rather, that it can really avoid such determinism only by rejecting the linguistic monism that Butler seems to endorse, and by going back to a Foucaultian view that emphasizes the role of both discursive and nondiscursive practices in the process of subjection.[56]

The third hesitation that I have about Butler's analysis has to do with the difficulty she has in theorizing collective resistance or solidarity—a difficulty that she shares with Foucault but, unlike some of the other difficulties with his analysis, that she fails to resolve. In order to be adequate to feminism's critical aims, a conception of power ought to be able to say something about the kind of power that nourishes collective oppositional social movements such as the feminist movement, and that sustains coalitions between this movement and other social movements such as the gay rights movement, the anti-racism movement, new labor movements, and so on. One consequence of Butler's radical critique of identity and identity politics is that it becomes difficult to conceptualize such collective power. Indeed, it becomes difficult even to conceptualize collectivity at all. Near the end of *Bodies That Matter*, Butler returns to the problematic category of women with which *Gender Trouble* began. It is necessary, Butler concedes, to invoke the category of "women," but we must at the same time continue to challenge and question this category, "perpetually to interrogate the exclusions by which it proceeds."[57]

Butler's hesitant avowal of the category of "women" makes it difficult to see how one could theorize the kind of collective power that sustains and nourishes the feminist movement—a movement that presses its demands in the name of women: namely, the power of solidarity. Indeed, Butler assumes that solidarity is inextricably linked to problematic notions of unity or identity; thus, she contends that solidarity is "an exclusionary norm . . . that rules out the possibility of a set of actions which disrupt the very borders of identity concepts."[58] Allison Weir sums up the problem with Butler's linking of solidarity with exclusion: On such a view, Weir writes, "it becomes impossible to see the affirmations of existential and political identities which provide a sense of meaning and solidarity to participants in feminist, gay and lesbian, and black struggles for empowerment as anything other than paradoxical affirmations of the identitary logic of domination and exclusion."[59]

The problem is not just that Butler is suspicious of the notion of solidarity, for one might agree with her for the sake of argument that this term is too loaded with presumptions of original unity to be part of a contemporary political vocabulary. Even more problematic is her suspicion of consensus or agreement per se. She writes, "The ideal of consent . . . makes sense only to the degree that the terms in question submit to a consensually established meaning. . . . But are we, whoever 'we' are, the kind of community in which such meanings could be established once and for all? . . . Who stands above the interpretive fray in a position to 'assign' utterances the same meanings?"[60] Thus, in Butler's view, dialogic models of collective action and identification run the risk of "relapsing into a liberal model that assumes that speaking agents occupy equal positions of power and speak with the same presuppositions about what constitutes 'agreement' and 'unity' and, indeed, that those are the goals to be sought."[61]

The problem is that this suspicion of consensus allows Butler to leave untheorized crucial domains of social analysis. As Jodi Dean puts it, theories such as Butler's

> cannot account for the positive and communicative dimensions of our lives. Not only are microdisruptions and performative reiterations hardly enough to challenge the continued brutalization of women in their homes, the reinvigorated homophobia of the Right, and the continued economic exploitation of women across the globe, but such disruptions and reiterations themselves, as their theorists admit, can backfire, either manipulated by their opponents or coopted into new practices of violence.[62]

Dean fails to acknowledge that communicative agreements might also backfire; nevertheless, she is correct in noting that Butler's suspicion of such agreements makes the theory of performativity fall short of providing an analysis of the collective empowerment that grows out of the feminist movement and, in turn, serves as a resource for individual women who are struggling with heterosexist domination in their daily lives.[63] Further, this suspicion, coupled with Butler's uneasiness about normative concepts, makes it difficult, if not impossible, to maintain important distinctions between normatively beneficial and normatively problematic forms of collective action, between agreements based on persuasion, bargaining, and genuine overlapping of interests, and those based on coercion, intimidation, and brute force.[64]

This failure is evident in Butler's analysis of gay activism. Activist projects such as cross-dressing, gay pride parades, ACT UP's die-ins, and Queer Nation's kiss-ins are analyzed solely as instances of hyperbolic performativity that destabilize the naturalness of heterosexist gender norms.[65] Although it is certainly interesting and productive to view such projects through this theoretical lens, it is also possible and, indeed, necessary to analyze them as instances of consensual, reciprocal action that are possible because of a collective empowerment on the part of participants, which in turn sustains such action and serves as an important normative resource for individuals struggling against the hegemony of heterosexism.

Conclusion

In conclusion, let me sum up the strengths and weaknesses of Butler's feminist appropriation and extension of Foucault's analysis of power. First, the strengths: Her account resolves the Foucaultian paradox of agency by introducing the notion of citationality as that which mediates between individual subjects and the oppressive sex/gender norms to which they are subjected; as a result of her resolution of this paradox, Butler is also able to provide a more satisfactory account of resistance than Foucault. In sum, Butler builds on Foucault's conceptual insights into the interplay between constraint and enablement, between power-over and power-to, and, more important, she does so in a way that avoids some of the more serious conceptual shortcomings of Foucault's own account.

However, as I have argued, significant weaknesses remain. First, Butler fails to ground her implicit normative judgments in the necessary normative framework. Although Butler is willing to admit that there might be a normative dimension to her theory of performativity, her suspicion of normativity per se leaves her open to the charge that she neglects to explain why anyone should feel compelled to carry out the performative denaturalization of sex that she calls for. I think that this limitation can be addressed, however, without going too far out of the bounds of Butler's theoretical framework; it is a matter of owning up to the normative demands that are already implicit in her analysis and offering defenses of those demands, while still viewing the demands themselves as contingent and essentially contested.

Second, unlike Foucault, Butler focuses too narrowly on the discursive dimensions of power, and subsumes all of what Foucault might have regarded as nondiscursive practices under the all-encompassing umbrella of discourse. This narrow focus leads her to portray discourse as both all-powerful and yet strangely impotent. It strikes me that this limitation can be addressed by pushing Butler back toward her Foucaultian roots and reemphasizing the role that nondiscursive, bodily practices play alongside discursive practices in the Foucaultian analysis of power on which her theory of performativity is based.

Finally, like Foucault, Butler seems to presume a strategic conception of power that renders her analysis blind to the kind of collective power that makes feminist solidarity possible. Whereas the first two limitations to Butler's analysis of power can be addressed from within a Foucaultian framework, the third limitation can be remedied only by going beyond a Foucaultian/Butlerian framework for analyzing power altogether. In order to make sense of the collective use of power that I call feminist solidarity, we shall have to reject the assumption that power is always and only exercised in strategic ways. I shall call this assumption into question in a more thorough way in Chapter 4 by way of a consideration of what might seem at first glance to be a radically different, perhaps even philosophically incompatible, analysis of power: that of Hannah Arendt.

In order to be adequate to feminism's critical aims, we require a conception of power that moves beyond the limitations of the feminist conceptions of power that I discussed in Chapter 1. Although there are some limitations in Butler's account that will need to be overcome, her work takes significant strides in this direction. Whereas her early formulation of performativity remains too faithful to Foucault's analysis of power and, thus, founders on the determinism/voluntarism divide and fails to offer a satisfactory account of agency, the introduction in her more recent work of the concept of citationality allows her to deftly negotiate the complicated dialectical interplay between domination and resistance. Thus, despite its blind spots, the theory of performativity makes a significant contribution to a feminist conception of power. Moreover, that there are blind spots in her account would probably come as no surprise to Butler. As she writes in the introduction to *Bodies That Matter*, the "demand to think contemporary power in its complexity and interarticulations remains incontrovertibly important *even in its impossibility*."[66] To her credit, Butler is so convinced of the importance of the task and the demand to attempt it that she is willing to run the risk of meeting up with its impossibility.

Notes

1. Judith Butler, *Gender Trouble: Feminism and the Subversion of Identity* (New York: Routledge, 1990).

2. Judith Butler, *Bodies That Matter: On the Discursive Limits of "Sex"* (New York: Routledge, 1993).

3. Judith Butler, *Excitable Speech: A Politics of the Performative* (New York: Routledge, 1997).

4. Seyla Benhabib, Judith Butler, Drucilla Cornell, and Nancy Fraser, *Feminist Contentions: A Philosophical Exchange* (New York: Routledge, 1995).

5. Butler, *Gender Trouble*, p. 2.

6. Ibid., p. 5; emphasis Butler's.

7. Two exceptions who come to mind are Jane Flax, who has a conception of the priority of sex over gender similar to Butler's, and (perhaps surprisingly) Catharine MacKinnon, whose claim that all differences are simply the reified effects of dominance can easily be interpreted to cover sex differences as well as gender differences. See Jane Flax, *Thinking Fragments: Psychoanalysis, Feminism, and Postmodernism in the Contemporary West* (Berkeley: University of California Press, 1990); and Catharine MacKinnon, "Difference and Dominance: On Sex Discrimination," in MacKinnon, *Feminism Unmodified* (Cambridge, Mass.: Harvard University Press, 1987).

8. Butler, *Gender Trouble*, p. 7. See also pp. 106–111 for an extended critique of scientific attempts to explain the naturalness of sex differences.

9. Ibid., p. 25.

10. Ibid., p. 124.

11. Ibid.

12. Allison Weir, *Sacrificial Logics: Feminist Theory and the Critique of Identity* (New York: Routledge, 1996), p. 113.

13. "In an application that Nietzsche himself would not have anticipated or condoned, we might state as a corollary: There is no gender identity behind the expressions of gender; that identity is performatively constituted by the very 'expressions' that are said to be its results" (Butler, *Gender Trouble*, p. 25).

14. Seyla Benhabib, "Feminism and Postmodernism: An Uneasy Alliance," in Benhabib et al., *Feminist Contentions*, p. 21.

15. Susan Bordo, "Postmodern Subjects, Postmodern Bodies, Postmodern Resistance," in Bordo, *Unbearable Weight* (Berkeley: University of California Press, 1993), p. 292.

16. Ibid., pp. 293–294.

17. Ibid., p. 294.

18. Butler, *Gender Trouble*, p. 2.

19. Cf. Allison Weir's similar claim that *Gender Trouble* "provides no account of a process of mediation between norms and acts" (Weir, *Sacrificial Logics*, p. 122). However, Weir implies—incorrectly, I think—that this lack of mediation between norms and acts also characterizes Butler's work in *Bodies That Matter*. As I shall

argue in the next section, the major advance of *Bodies That Matter* is that it does provide such an account of mediation with the notion of citationality or iterability.

20. Butler, *Bodies That Matter*, p. x.

21. Ibid.

22. See ibid., p. xii. To be sure, the determinism/voluntarism problem is not the only difficulty that Butler's reformulation of performativity is designed to resolve. For instance, *Bodies That Matter* also addresses at length the objection that the theory of performativity fails to take into account the materiality of the body (see *Bodies That Matter*, passim). More recently, Butler addresses the worry that *Gender Trouble* failed to take into account the psychic workings of gender that may not be evident in the performance of that gender (see Judith Butler, *The Psychic Life of Power: Theories in Subjection* [Stanford, Calif.: Stanford University Press, 1997], pp. 144ff.).

23. Benhabib, "Feminism and Postmodernism," in Benhabib et al., *Feminist Contentions*, p. 21. Butler seems to think that Benhabib willfully misreads her work and "chooses not to consider what meaning of performativity is at work [in *Gender Trouble*]" (see Butler, "For a Careful Reading," in Benhabib et al., *Feminist Contentions*, p. 134). However, this interpretation seems unfair to Benhabib given the fact that Butler does not provide a clear account of the theoretical roots of her usage of performativity in her earliest formulations of the theory.

24. Jacques Derrida, "Signature, Event, Context," in Gerald Graff, ed., *Limited, Inc.*, trans. Samuel Weber and Jeffrey Mehlman (Evanston: Northwestern University Press, 1988), p. 18. Quoted in Butler, "For a Careful Reading," in Benhabib et al., *Feminist Contentions*, p. 134; in Butler, *Bodies That Matter*, p. 13; and in Butler, *Excitable Speech*, p. 51.

25. Butler, *Bodies That Matter*, p. 95.

26. Ibid., p. 108.

27. Elsewhere, Butler acknowledges that seeing *Paris Is Burning* prompted her to rethink the claim that parody always entails subversion. See the discussion in John Rajchman, ed., *The Identity in Question* (New York: Routledge, 1995), p. 134.

28. On this point, see Butler, *Bodies That Matter*, p. 125.

29. See Bordo, "Postmodern Subjects, Postmodern Bodies, Postmodern Resistance," pp. 292–294; and Fraser, "False Antitheses," in Benhabib et al., *Feminist Contentions*, p. 68.

30. Butler, *Bodies That Matter*, p. 95.

31. Butler, *Excitable Speech*, p. 160.

32. Butler, *Bodies That Matter*, p. 231.

33. Ibid., p. 237.

34. Butler, *The Psychic Life of Power*, pp. 1–2. Cf. Butler, *Bodies That Matter*, p. 15. For Foucault's formulations of this paradox, see Michel Foucault, "Afterword: The Subject and Power," in Hubert Dreyfus and Paul Rabinow, *Michel Foucault: Beyond Structuralism and Hermeneutics* (Chicago: University of Chicago Press, 1982); and Michel Foucault, *Discipline and Punish: The Birth of the Prison*, trans. Alan Sheridan (New York: Vintage, 1979). In *The Psychic Life of Power*, Butler takes a markedly different approach to the question of subjection, an approach that attempts to bring together the insights of Freudian psychoanalysis and a Foucault-

ian analysis of power. Because this approach differs substantially from the one that I have been discussing, a full account of it is beyond the scope of this chapter.

35. Butler, *Bodies That Matter*, p. 22.

36. See Butler, *Excitable Speech*, pp. 65–66.

37. Ibid., p. 67.

38. Ibid., p. 68.

39. Ibid., p. 69.

40. Butler, *Bodies That Matter*, pp. 21–22.

41. Butler, "Contingent Foundations," in Benhabib et al., *Feminist Contentions*, p. 50; emphasis added.

42. Fraser, "False Antitheses," p. 71.

43. Butler, *Bodies That Matter*, p. 125; emphasis added.

44. Ibid., p. 131.

45. Fraser, "Pragmatism, Feminism, and the Linguistic Turn," in Benhabib et al., *Feminist Contentions*, p. 162.

46. Allison Weir makes a similar point in her discussion of Butler's critique of language as identitarian. Such a claim, Weir notes, rests on the presupposition that language always misrepresents the plurality and nonidentity that *really* exist. (See Weir, *Sacrificial Logics*, pp. 118–120.)

47. Butler, *Bodies That Matter*, p. 2.

48. Ibid.

49. Ibid., p. 11; emphasis added.

50. Ibid., p. 23.

51. Jacqueline Zita, Review of *Bodies That Matter, Signs* 21:3 (1996): 794.

52. Butler, *Bodies That Matter*, p. 8.

53. Ibid., p. 10.

54. Butler, *Excitable Speech*, p. 21.

55. Ibid., p. 108; emphasis added.

56. On this point, see Bordo, "Postmodern Subjects, Postmodern Bodies, Postmodern Resistance," pp. 291–292.

57. Butler, *Bodies That Matter*, p. 222.

58. Butler, *Gender Trouble*, p. 15.

59. Weir, *Sacrificial Logics*, pp. 113–114.

60. Butler, *Excitable Speech*, pp. 86–87. Butler's target in this passage is Jürgen Habermas's theory of communicative action, which she seems to misinterpret. She cites the following passage from Habermas: "The productivity of the process of understanding remains unproblematic only as long as all participants stick to the reference point of possibly achieving a mutual understanding in which the *same* utterances are assigned the same meaning" (Jürgen Habermas, *The Philosophical Discourse of Modernity*, trans. Frederick J. Lawrence [Cambridge, Mass.: MIT Press, 1987], p. 198; quoted in Butler, *Excitable Speech*, p. 87). In this passage, it seems clear that Habermas is interested only in the *possibility* of achieving mutual understanding and that it is this possibility (counterfactually imputed into discourse) that serves as a "reference point" or regulative ideal for communication. See Barbara Fultner, "Habermas and Butler on Universality and Idealisation," paper presented at the Fifth Annual Critical Theory Roundtable, St. Louis University, September 26–28, 1997.

61. Butler, *Gender Trouble*, p. 15.

62. Jodi Dean, *Solidarity of Strangers: Feminism After Identity Politics* (Berkeley: University of California Press, 1996), p. 66.

63. For an account of how the normative and social resources generated by the women's movement serve as resources for individual women (even women who do not identify themselves as feminists), see Jane Mansbridge, "The Role of Discourse in the Feminist Movement," paper presented at the American Political Science Association annual meeting, September 2–5, 1993.

64. For a similar argument against Derrida, see Thomas McCarthy, "The Politics of the Ineffable: Derrida's Deconstructionism," in McCarthy, *Ideals and Illusions: On Reconstruction and Deconstruction in Contemporary Critical Theory* (Cambridge, Mass.: MIT Press, 1991), p. 110; and against Foucault, see Nancy Fraser, "Foucault on Modern Power: Empirical Insights and Normative Confusions," in Fraser, *Unruly Practices*, p. 32.

65. For a somewhat different account of die-ins, one that understands them as ways of staging the melancholic grief that is culturally proscribed for the loss of homosexual love, see Butler, *The Psychic Life of Power*, pp. 147–148. Although Butler refers to the die-ins here as "collective institutions for grieving" (p. 148), she nevertheless falls short of understanding them as a source of collective empowerment based on the consensual, reciprocal action of the participants.

66. Butler, *Bodies That Matter*, p. 19; emphasis added.

4

The Power of Solidarity:
Hannah Arendt

Drawing on the work of Hannah Arendt for feminist purposes involves treading on dangerous, and continually shifting, ground. For although there has recently been something of an Arendt renaissance among feminist theorists, the implications of her political theory for oppositional social movements such as feminism are far from clear.[1] Arendt purposefully evaded "the woman problem," steadfastly refused to identify herself with the feminist movement, and relegated any discussion of women and their position in the *vita activa* to the footnotes of her monumental work, *The Human Condition*. And although she wasn't as evasive about race, the way she dealt with it may well make her admirers wish that she was: Her extremely negative portrayal of the black student movement and her public opposition to federally enforced desegregation in the South make it difficult to see how her political theory can have anything productive to say to theorists who are interested in challenging racism.[2] Finally, given Arendt's desire to keep the body and its needs, wants, and desires out of the public, political sphere and in the private world of labor, it is easy to conclude that Arendt tacitly rejects the possibility of a politics of sexuality.[3]

These difficulties might well be intractable if my goal here was to evaluate the implications of Arendt's work as a whole from the perspective of feminist theory, critical race theory, or queer theory, or if it was to explore the nascent feminism, critical race theory, or queer theory in her work.[4] Although these might be interesting and important ways of thinking about her work, I approach the intersection of Arendt and feminist theory from another direction. My focus is on the theoretical resources that we can cull from Arendt's work that might then be put to use in a feminist conception of power designed to illuminate the intersecting axes of domination and subordination based on gender, race, class, and sexuality, and to highlight the possibilities for individual and collective resistance to such domination. Specifically, I shall argue that Arendt offers a view of power that can help us to thematize the solidary ties that bind members of social movements together and thus make collective resistance possible. Moreover, I shall argue that an Arendtian account of solidarity is particularly appealing because it does not rely on essentialist and, thus, exclusionary notions of group identity. Instead, the account of solidarity that can be culled from Arendt's work grows out of the dialectical interplay between identity and nonidentity, between equality and distinction, that is at the heart of Arendt's understanding of political life. Thus, Arendt's account of power fills in a lacuna in the analysis offered by Foucault and Butler, both of whom I criticized in previous chapters for ignoring the power of solidarity; and, more important, it does so in a way that avoids the problematic essentialism that Butler finds objectionable in traditional feminist accounts of solidarity.

Foucault, Butler, and Arendt:
An Unlikely Alliance

But this attempt to bring an Arendtian account of power together with the analysis developed by Foucault and Butler gives rise to a new set of difficulties, for one might assume that Arendt, on the one hand, and Foucault and Butler, on the other, are on entirely different philosophical planes. Thus, one might be highly suspicious of any attempt to integrate their insights into the study of power. Indeed, the obvious philosophical differences between these theorists might, for instance, make it all the more surprising that, toward the end of *Excitable Speech*, Butler points out an affinity between her work and that of Arendt. Butler claims that her analysis of injurious speech constitutes an extension of the claim, made by political theorists such as Arendt, "that it is as *linguistic* that humans become political kinds of beings."[5] Indeed, Arendt makes this claim more than once. For instance, in *On Revolution*, she claims that "man, to the extent that he is a political being, is endowed with the power of speech. The two famous definitions of man by Aristotle, that he is a political being [*zoon politikon*] and a being endowed with speech [*zoon logon ekhon*], supplement each other and both refer to the same experience in Greek *polis* life."[6] The affinity between Butler and Arendt on this point seems clear enough, but it might be surprising that such a similarity exists, or that Butler bothers to point it out. After all, one might ordinarily assume that Arendt and Butler would have little in common philosophically. Indeed, this assumption, if true, could potentially cause trouble for the line of argument that I am pursuing in this book. For if it is true that Arendt on the one hand and Butler (and Foucault) on the other have radically different philosophical views, then my attempt to draw on the insights of all three thinkers to formulate a feminist conception of power could be accused of bringing together inconsistent or, worse, contradictory philosophical frameworks.

I think, however, that the contrast between Arendt and Foucault and Butler is overdrawn. After all, Arendt's philosophical lineage must be traced not only through Aristotle, Augustine, and Kant but also through Nietzsche and Heidegger;[7] the latter influences surely draw her nearer to Foucault[8] and thus, indirectly, to Butler. Indeed, Seyla Benhabib has argued persuasively that there is a fundamental tension in Arendt's political thought between her modernist commitment to universal morality and her "postmodernist" critique of foundationalism; as a result of this tension, Benhabib labels Arendt a "reluctant modernist."[9] If Benhabib is correct, then despite Arendt's commitment to some of the ideals of modernity, there are elements of her thought that are compatible with a postmodernist perspective such as Foucault's and Butler's. In order to allay the worries raised above about the compatibility of these two philosophical frameworks, I shall preface my discussion of Arendt's conception of power with a consideration of the similarities and differences between those frameworks.

First, the similarities.

1. Foucault, Butler, and Arendt are all sharply critical of Hegelian/ Marxist dialectical philosophy of history on the grounds that it implies that nothing totally new and unexpected can happen. Foucault develops this critique in his early, archaeological works. For instance, *The Order of Things* is generally interpreted as introducing an anti-Hegelian philosophy of history that emphasizes rupture and discontinuity over reconciliation and dialectical continuity.[10] Similarly, in the Introduction to *The Archaeology of Knowledge*, Foucault positions himself against Hegelian philosophy of history by claiming that his aim in that book

> is most decidedly not to use the categories of cultural totalities (whether world-views, ideal types, the particular spirit of an age) in order to impose on history, despite itself, the forms of structural analysis. The series described, the limits fixed, the comparisons and correlations made are based not on the old philosophies of history, but are intended to question teleologies and totalizations.[11]

In her first book, *Subjects of Desire: Hegelian Reflections in Twentieth-Century France*, Butler indicates that she agrees with this Foucaultian critique of Hegelian philosophy of history: "Foucault's analysis of modernity attempts to show how the terms of dialectical opposition do not resolve into more synthetic and inclusive terms but tend instead to splinter off

into a multiplicity of terms which expose the dialectic itself as a limited
methodological tool for historians."[12]

Arendt's critique of Hegelian philosophy of history likewise centers on
its emphasis on the dialectical continuity and necessity of history. According to Arendt, the problem with this view is that it fails to ring true
when it is measured against our recent history. In Arendt's view, all of the
experiences of the twentieth century in the West—most notably the Holo-
caust of European Jewry and the explosion of the atomic bombs at Hi-
roshima and Nagasaki—have "confronted us with the totally unexpected."[13] Indeed, Arendt suggests that the very popularity of this view
of history "seems to consist in offering a comfortable, speculative or
pseudo-scientific refuge from reality."[14] Seyla Benhabib points out that
Arendt's discontinuous historiography is motivated by her study of the
emergence of totalitarianism. Above all, Benhabib claims, Arendt does
not want to make totalitarianism out to be a historical necessity; thus, her
approach in *The Origins of Totalitarianism* is to "break the chain of narrative continuity, to shatter chronology as the natural structure of narrative,
to stress fragmentariness, historical dead ends, failures, and ruptures."[15]
Arendt's rejection of the Hegelian model is further evidenced by her interest in natality, in the beginning anew that is attendant upon all political action and that is found in its purest, most radical form in political
revolution.[16] Because her interest is in the capacity to begin something
anew—that is, the capacity for action—Arendt rejects the Hegelian claim
that "nothing but the 'necessary' results of what we already know . . .
that, in Hegel's words, 'nothing else will come out but what was already
there.'"[17] Thus, Foucault, Butler, and Arendt all share a critique of
Hegelian philosophy of history and an attempt to rethink the historical
such that it can account for ruptures, discontinuities, dead ends, and radically new beginnings.

2. Foucault and Arendt also share a critique of the normalizing power
of modern society.[18] Foucault's critique of normalization is well known. It
emerges out of his analyses of the disciplinary techniques employed by
psychiatrists, prison officials, doctors, judges, educators, and parents; the
aim of these techniques is to isolate, examine, modify, and normalize the
behavior of the perverts, delinquents, and madmen (or potential perverts, delinquents, and madmen) under their charge. Arendt's critique of
normalization emerges out of her critique of the rise in the modern era of
the domain of the social, a hybrid sphere that results from bringing the
private concerns of the household into the public sphere of politics. According to Arendt, the rise of the social coincides with the advent of mass
culture, and mass culture functions through normalization. Thus, she
notes, with the rise of mass culture, society comes to expect certain kinds
of behavior from individuals, and to impose "numerable and various

rules, all of which tend to 'normalize' its members, to make them behave, to exclude spontaneous action or outstanding achievement."[19] For Arendt, then, normalization is problematic because it inculcates a conformism that discourages individuals from beginning anew and, thus, from acting in the political sphere at all.[20]

3. In the works written shortly before their deaths, both Foucault and Arendt turn to aesthetics to develop a model of ethical or political judgment. In *The Use of Pleasure*, volume two of the *History of Sexuality*, Foucault examines the ethical *rapport a soi* that characterized ancient Greek life. The ethics that emerged out of this Greek relation to self took the form of an aesthetics of existence; the elite among the Greeks pursued an ethical/aesthetic ideal, striving to "live a beautiful life, and to leave to others memories of a beautiful existence."[21] Although Foucault is quite clear that he is not holding up the Greek aesthetics of existence as a laudable alternative to modern, normalizing, disciplinary societies, he nevertheless hints that we might find in this way of life clues for how best to rethink ethics in the secular, post-traditional West. Thus, he indicates that his own ethical view is modeled on the aesthetic. Similarly, in her *Lectures on Kant's Political Philosophy*, Arendt develops a model of political judgment that is based on Kant's notion of aesthetic judgment.[22] Already in *The Human Condition*, Arendt had drawn an analogy between acting in the public sphere and acting on a stage; theater, Arendt contends, is the "political art par excellence," for only in theater is "the political sphere of human life transposed into art."[23] Elsewhere, Arendt takes this analogy further, claiming that art and politics are related in that "both are phenomena of the public world"; Kant's analytic of the beautiful in the *Critique of Judgment* introduces a model of aesthetic judgment that "implies a political rather than a merely theoretical activity"—namely, the activity of exercising an "enlarged mentality" and "thinking in the place of everybody else."[24] Kant's notion of aesthetic judgment thus forms the basis for the account of political judgment that Arendt was developing at the time of her death.[25]

4. Foucault, Butler, and Arendt also share a critique of the humanist and existentialist notion of subjectivity, which views human subjects as autonomous, self-created, rational agents set over and against the social, cultural, and historical forces of their world. As was made clear in Chapters 2 and 3, Foucault and Butler reject this understanding of subjectivity in favor of an account of subjection, which views human subjects as effects of the power/knowledge regimes to which they are subject. Similarly, Arendt rejects the existentialist and humanist notion of subjectivity, claiming that "all notions of man creating himself have in common a rebellion against the very factuality of the human condition—nothing is more obvious than that man . . . does *not* owe his existence to himself."[26]

At times, Arendt even speaks of the subject as subjected in something close to Foucault's and Butler's sense of that term. For instance, she claims that the results of action and speech in the political realm are recorded in the life stories of the actors who participate in public life. However, "nobody is the author or producer of his own life story. . . . Somebody began it and is its subject *in the twofold sense of the word, namely, its actor and sufferer*, but nobody is its author."[27]

Recently, commentators have noted this continuity between Arendt's post-humanist account of subjectivity and Foucault's and Butler's account. For instance, Bonnie Honig has argued that, for Arendt, taking up the position of a political subject is always a performative act: One is not a political subject in advance of acting; rather, one becomes a subject by appearing and acting in the public sphere. As Honig describes it, this conception of subjectivity sounds strikingly similar to the conception offered in Butler's theory of performativity:

> The conception of the self presupposed in [Arendt] is an agonistic, differentiated, multiple, non-identitied being that is always becoming, always calling out for augmentation and amendment. And the politics truest to all this is likewise agonistic . . . and performative, potentially subversive, and always seeking to create new relations and establish new realities.[28]

Although I suspect that Honig overemphasizes the postmodern side of Arendt here, she is right to note this dimension of Arendt's conception of subjectivity; and this dimension has clear affinities with the socially constructed account of subjectivity embraced by both Foucault and Butler.

5. Finally, for the purposes of this book, undoubtedly the most important broad similarity between Arendt, Foucault, and Butler is that they all reject the juridical or command-obedience model of power.[29] As was discussed in detail in Chapters 2 and 3, Foucault and Butler reject this model on the grounds that it neglects the productive aspects of power. Arendt, by contrast, criticizes this model on the grounds that it misconstrues the nature of politics and, thus, denies the very possibility of political action. According to Arendt, the juridical model of power presupposes that human beings can coexist in a political community only when some command and others are obedient; for her, this belief represents an "escape from the frailty of human affairs into the solidity of quiet and order."[30] In Arendt's view, the escapism of the command-obedience model is motivated by the messiness and uncertainty attendant on action in the public, political realm. In her view, there is a "haphazardness and moral irresponsibility inherent in a plurality of agents."[31] As a result, action in the public, political realm is always marked by three frustrating characteristics: Its outcome is unpredictable, so it tends to produce unintended ef-

fects; as a result of this, once an action has been initiated, it is irreversible; and, as a result of these first two characteristics, the author of an action is often unknown.[32] Arendt contends that political theorists since Plato have attempted to circumvent these frustrations by substituting the stability of the rule of some over others for the uncertainty of collective action. However, the problem with this substitution, according to Arendt, is that it entails no less than an escape from politics itself. Against this escapism, Arendt ultimately introduced a conception of power that embraces both the uncertainty and the promise of collective political action.

Thus, by challenging the command-obedience model of power as sovereignty, Foucault, Butler, and Arendt all strive to cut off the head of the king. Furthermore, all three reject this model in favor of an understanding of power as something that is not held or possessed (by a sovereign or anyone else), but that is fundamentally relational. As we have seen, both Foucault and Butler maintain that "power is not something that is acquired, seized, or shared, something that one holds on to or allows to slip away; power is exercised."[33] In a similar vein, Arendt claims that power exists only by being actualized; power is not a thing or a stuff that one might possess. In Arendt's view, power "springs up between men when they act together and vanishes the moment they disperse."[34]

To be sure, Foucault and Butler, on the one hand, and Arendt, on the other, take their rejections of the command-obedience model and the relational conceptions of power to which they lead in quite different directions. Foucault and Butler, as we have seen, reject the juridical model in favor of a more sinister and ominous account of the way that power produces the very subjects that it constrains. According to them, power is not just exercised in the commands of the sovereign or of the law; it is in our bodies, our heads, even in our hearts. Arendt, by contrast, rejects that model in favor of a more positive, perhaps even overly optimistic, understanding of power as the capacity to act in concert. Although it would be impossible to deny the differences in direction taken by these approaches to the study of power, my suggestion is that we might view such differences as complementary rather than contradictory.

This brings me to the major philosophical differences between Foucault, Butler, and Arendt.

1. As discussed above, Foucault fails to make crucial normative distinctions between different ways of exercising power; indeed, in light of the fact that his genealogical studies expose the sinister side of norms themselves, it is difficult to see how he might make such normative distinctions. Although Butler is at times willing to gesture hesitantly toward a normative dimension in her analysis, she nonetheless fails to provide the kind of normative framework that could ground her own call for a denaturalization of sex. Arendt, by contrast, accepts precisely the kind of uni-

versalistic normative framework that Foucault and Butler reject. Benhabib summarizes Arendt's normative position as follows:

> Hannah Arendt was a reluctant modernist, but a modernist nonetheless, who
> celebrated the universal declaration of the rights of man and citizen; who took
> it for granted that women were entitled to the same political and civic rights
> as men; who denounced imperialist ventures in Egypt, India, South Africa,
> and Palestine; who did not mince words in her critique of the bourgeoisie and
> of capitalism, or in her condemnation of modern nationalist movements.[35]

Thus, Arendt employs just the sort of normative critique of which Foucault and Butler remain highly suspicious.

Furthermore, Arendt's normative framework is built into her conception of power itself. Arendt not only rejects the command-obedience model of power on the grounds that it is fundamentally apolitical, she also rejects it on normative grounds. If one equates power, as those who accept the command-obedience model do, with the ability to get others to do what one wishes, then it follows that violence is the ultimate form that power can take. Arendt's worry here is that if power is viewed simply as the effectiveness of command, then it becomes difficult to differentiate between legitimate and illegitimate types of commands; in her view, the command-obedience model views violence as a particular way of exercising power and treats both as normatively neutral phenomena. Arendt, as we shall see, remedies this problem by building normative criteria into her definition of power itself.

To be sure, the foregoing represents a significant difference between Arendt, on the one hand, and Foucault and Butler, on the other; however, it does not pose a serious problem for my attempt to draw on all three of these theorists to formulate a feminist conception of power. On the contrary, I think that Arendt actually can provide the necessary corrective to Foucault's and Butler's "normative confusions," to borrow Nancy Fraser's phrase. I argued above that the account of power that emerged out of my consideration of Foucault and Butler would need to be supplemented with the kind of normative framework that can ground feminist critique; given the other broad similarities between Arendt and Foucault and Butler, her conception of power seems to be an excellent candidate for providing such a framework (or at least certain elements of it).

2. Whereas Foucault and Butler reject the notion that the operation of power is confined to the goings on of the public, political sphere and challenge the very distinction between public and private by arguing that power—traditionally regarded as a political concept that is irrelevant for discussions of the private sphere—permeates the social body, Arendt laments the collapsing of the distinction between private and

public spheres and the resulting rise of the social, reasserts a strict meta-physical distinction between the two, and insists that the public is the only sphere in which power operates. Arendt's adherence to this distinc-tion is the result of what Seyla Benhabib has labeled her "phenomenolog-ical essentialism," a view that commits her to the "belief that each human activity has its proper place and can only reveal its essence properly in that place."[36] According to Arendt, the public sphere is the space of poli-tics in which people act collectively and, thus—since Arendt understands power as the human capacity to act collectively—exercise power. The pri-vate sphere, by contrast, is the apolitical realm of necessity, in which life is produced and reproduced. Because Arendt asserted a strict distinction between these two spheres, she also argued that bringing private domes-tic concerns under the jurisdiction of politics violates the proper order of the human condition and, hence, is undesirable and potentially danger-ous. It is dangerous because, according to Arendt, the private sphere is also the sphere of violence, for violence is necessary for the mastering of necessity and nature that go on in private. Thus, when private issues are addressed with political means, political power can degenerate quickly into violence.[37] In recent history, private concerns have been brought in-creasingly into the public sphere; the result of this has been the rise of the "social." This outcome is worrisome to Arendt because she believes that the social threatens to destroy the sanctity of both the public and the pri-vate spheres; it obeys "an irresistible tendency to grow, to devour the older realms of the political and private,"[38] and, as was mentioned above, its rise is accompanied by an increase in normalization and a resulting decrease in the spontaneity and distinction that characterize politics for Arendt.

The crux of the difference between Arendt and Foucault and Butler on this point has to do not so much with their analyses of the interpenetra-tion of public and private realms and the resultant rise of the social as with their reaction to this phenomenon. Although it would seem strangely out of character for Foucault or Butler to characterize the rise of the social in positive terms, they clearly do not share Arendt's alarm over this historical development nor do they share her desire to reinstate a strict, quasi-metaphysical separation between public and private. In short, Arendt's phenomenological essentialism seems to introduce some metaphysical baggage that Foucault and Butler surely would reject. This difficulty must be addressed if I am to successfully integrate their con-ceptions of power.

Specifically, in order to address this problem, I must strip Arendt's con-ception of action and power of its metaphysical baggage. Seyla Benhabib has suggested a way of reading with Arendt/against Arendt that enables us to jettison the more troubling metaphysical aspects of her distinction among the public, the private, and the social. Benhabib delineates three different ways that Arendt draws the distinction between the public and the social. The first takes these terms to refer to different object domains; in this way of drawing the distinction, debates about economic distribution, for instance, would be considered social, whereas debates about constitutional interpretation would be deemed political. Benhabib argues that this way of drawing the distinction is unacceptable, however, because it obscures the power relations that underlie the economic domain. As she puts it, the issues raised by economic—and, we might add, personal and familial—relations "can easily become political, in the emphatic Arendtian sense of raising fundamental questions about our life together as a collectivity of citizens."[39] The second way that this distinction can be drawn is along institutional lines. When these terms are distinguished in this way, "social" refers to the institutions of the economy and civil society, whereas "political" denotes the public sphere and the legal and political institutions of the state. However, this way of drawing the distinction is also inadequate, according to Benhabib, because Arendt's conception of public space is not "sophisticated and rich enough to do justice to the sociological complexity and variety of modern institutions."[40] For Benhabib, it is the third way of drawing this distinction that is the most promising: distinguishing between social and political along attitudinal rather than object-specific or institutional lines.[41] In this way of drawing the distinction, the social is marked by an attitude of narrow self-interest, whereas the political is characterized by an attitude of public or common interest. Arendt seems to presuppose this way of drawing the distinction when she claims that the social "is the form in which the fact of mutual dependence for the sake of life and nothing else assumes *public significance.*"[42] The same needs that are here framed as social can be formulated as political issues, however, if the attitude of self-interest is transformed into the political concern with issues of justice and the common interest. Arendt herself notes that this transformation occurred occasionally during the European Labor Movement, "in those rare and yet decisive moments when during the process of revolution it suddenly turned out that these people, if not led by official party programs and ideologies, had their own ideas about the possibilities of democratic government under modern conditions."[43] If the distinction is drawn in this way, then, Benhabib argues, "engaging in politics [for Arendt] does not mean abandoning economic or social issues; it means fighting for them in the name of principles, interests, values that have a generalizable basis, and that concern us as members of a collectivity."[44]

Although Arendt hints at an attitudinal distinction between the social and the political in her discussion of the Labor Movement, she is not consistent in drawing the distinction in this way. For instance, in her discussion of forced desegregation of schools in the South, Arendt leans on a more substantive, object-specific distinction between the social and the political, and with disastrous results.[45] Thus, reading Arendt in this way will involve revising parts of her theory in order to make use of the brilliance of her insights into power. Benhabib's revision of Arendt shows how her distinction between the social and the political can be stripped of its metaphysical baggage and, thus, brought together with the ardently anti-essentialist, post-metaphysical accounts of power offered by Foucault and Butler. Once we have stripped Arendt's distinction between the public and the social of its metaphysical baggage, we are free to accept Arendt's analysis of the rise of the social while rejecting the negative valence she attaches to it.[46] Doing so not only allows us to bring Arendt together with Foucault and Butler, but it also seems necessary for bringing Arendt's work to bear on feminist theory, critical race theory, and queer theory. After all, a good deal of feminist theory has consisted of bringing so-called private concerns such as reproduction, sexuality, familial relationships, and household work into public, political debate and exposing their political dimensions. Although Arendt herself was, as her biographer, Elizabeth Young-Bruehl notes, "steadfastly opposed to the social dimensions of 'Women's Liberation,'"[47] if we follow the attitudinal distinction between the public and the social that Arendt employs in her discussion of the Labor Movement, then it seems clear that feminist concerns about sexuality, family, household work, and so on can become political concerns in Arendt's sense so long as they are framed as issues about how to regulate our common life together as citizens. This strategy allows us to avoid some of the problems that Arendt runs into and also mitigates the difference between Arendt and Foucault and Butler on this point, since the latter two seem to share some aspects of her analysis of the interpenetration of private and public spheres in modern societies without sharing her alarm over this fact.

In sum, there are numerous similarities between Arendt and Foucault and Butler. And, although there are some significant differences between them as well, these differences are not insurmountable. With respect to the first difference, Arendt's reliance on a normative framework provides a much-needed corrective for the lack of normative distinctions in the work of Foucault and Butler. The second difference can be minimized by drawing on the less metaphysically loaded ways of distinguishing between the social and the political that are present, if underemphasized, in Arendt's own work. Given the broad similarities between Arendt and Foucault and Butler, and in light of the fact that the major differences can be mitigated in these ways, drawing on all three of these theorists in order to formulate a feminist conception of power seems to me to be entirely justified.

In the remainder of this chapter, then, I shall explore Arendt's thought with an eye toward seeing what it can contribute to a feminist analysis of power. I shall begin in the next section by discussing the key features of Arendt's conception of power and by laying out the distinctions she draws among power, violence, authority, and strength. In the third section, I go on to consider how this conception of power can be the basis of a new feminist conception of solidarity, a conception that avoids Butler's charge that solidarity is an exclusionary norm predicated on a notion of shared identity. Finally, in the concluding section, I address the limitations to Arendt's conception of power.

Arendt's Conception of Power

Arendt once claimed that "all our definitions are distinctions, . . . we are unable to say what anything is without distinguishing it from something else."[48] In light of this claim, it is perhaps most useful to begin our discussion of Arendt's understanding of power by explaining the distinctions she draws between power and related concepts such as violence, authority, and strength. This strategy will enable us to understand Arendt's theorization of power more deeply.

Above, I considered some of Arendt's reasons for rejecting the command-obedience model of power. A further reason for Arendt's rejection of this model is that it conflates power with violence, thus glossing over what she regards as a crucial distinction. Against this view, Arendt insists that it is violence, not power, that always involves a command-obedience relationship. Furthermore, according to Arendt, violence, unlike power, is always instrumental in character.[49] This means, first of all, that violence relies on instruments or implements—fists, weapons, armies—to back it up. Power, by contrast, relies not on instruments but on numbers: "Power always stands in need of numbers, whereas violence up to a point can manage without them because it relies on implements. . . . The extreme form of power is All against One, the extreme form of violence is One against All."[50] Second, the claim that violence is instrumental implies that, unlike power, it is a mere means to some end and, thus, can be justified only with reference to the end toward which it is directed. Power, by contrast, is an end in itself.[51] As an end in itself, power is, by its very nature, legitimate; its legitimacy is derived from the reciprocal, collective actions that give rise to power. Violence, by contrast, insofar as it is a mere means whose worth is always dependent on the end it serves, "can be justifiable, but it never will be legitimate."[52] Because violence relies on instruments, it is more durable and less fragile than power; since power, unlike violence, exists only when it is actualized, it cannot be stockpiled in the way that instruments of violence can be. Furthermore, as a result of the instrumental nature of violence, the danger inherent in it "will always be that the means overwhelm the end. If goals are not achieved rapidly, the result will be not merely defeat but the introduction of the practice of violence into the whole body politic."[53] Arendt diagnosed this tendency to pursue violence for its own sake rather than for the sake of some possibly noble end in the French Revolution's descent into terror and worried that it might lead the violent wing of the student movement in the late 1960s down the same path. According to Arendt, then, "power and violence are opposites; where the one rules absolutely, the other is absent."[54] However, more often than not power and violence are intermingled in the real world; they are analytically and conceptually distinct but in practice intertwined.

Like violence, authority involves a command-obedience relationship; in contrast to violence, however, authority does not rely on instruments of force to back it up. Instead, authority derives from a respect on the part of the one who is commanded for the bases of that authority; thus, the hallmark of authority "is unquestioning recognition by those who are asked to obey; neither coercion nor persuasion is needed."[55] Authority is often achieved by virtue of the attainment of a certain office or position. For instance, a devout Catholic obeys the commands of the pope simply out of respect for the pope's authority, which the pope enjoys by virtue of his position within the hierarchy of the Catholic church; as long as Catholics continue to respect the authority of the pope, he needs neither to coerce nor to cajole his subjects into obedience. Sometimes, however, a highly respected individual might attain a position of authority on his or her own. Thus, for instance, a well-respected member of a community might enjoy authority over others on the basis of her wisdom, her contributions to the good of the community, her personal integrity, and the like. Again, in practice, certain individuals may have access to both violence and authority. For example, the president of the United States is obeyed by many simply by virtue of their recognizing his authority; however, he also has access to an array of instruments of violence to ensure the effectiveness of his commands, should he need to avail himself of them. Insofar as authority is a command-obedience relationship, however, it is, like violence, fundamentally different from power.

Like violence and authority, strength also involves a command-obedience relationship. However, unlike violence, which depends on implements, and authority, which relies on the attainment of a certain status, strength is a property or characteristic that inheres in an individual, in some cases allows him or her to command, and convinces others that it is in their best interests to obey.[56] Thus, strength is distinguished from power both because it involves a command-obedience relationship and because it is the kind of thing that can be held or possessed by an individual. Power, by contrast, is a collective phenomenon: "Power is never the property of an individual; it belongs to a group and remains in existence only so long as the group keeps together."[57] Moreover, power cannot be held or possessed by groups either; it is not only a collective phenomenon but also a relational one. "In distinction to strength, which is the gift and the possession of every man in his isolation against all other men, power comes into being only if and when men join themselves together for the purpose of action; and it will disappear when, for whatever reason, they disperse and desert one another."[58] Finally, although strength might seem less ephemeral and more weighty than power, in reality the former is no match for the latter: "The strength of even the strongest individual can always be overpowered by the many, who often will combine for no other purpose than to ruin strength precisely because of its peculiar independence."[59]

From this set of distinctions, it is clear that power has, according to Arendt, the following characteristics: It is a collective, relational phenomenon that relies on numbers, not implements; it is an end in itself that is, thus, by its very nature legitimate; and, most important, its essence is not command or rule but collaboration and collective action. These characteristics are expressed succinctly in Arendt's definition of power as "the human ability not just to act but to act in concert."[60] In Arendt's view, power emerges from relationships between individuals who are working together for a common goal.

This conception of power cannot be understood fully, however, unless it is placed within the context of the other key terms in Arendt's political lexicon with which it is closely related: plurality, action, the public space, and promising. Since power is a collective phenomenon, it is the result of the irreducible plurality of human beings. Plurality, according to Arendt, is one of three fundamental aspects of the human condition. The first aspect of the human condition is biological life itself, the cyclical, biological processes of birth, growth, and death that characterize human life on earth. The second aspect is worldliness, which corresponds to the unnatural aspects of human existence, the worldly artifacts and things in which and by which we move. The final aspect is plurality, which corresponds to "the fact that men, not Man, live on the earth and inhabit the world."[61] Plurality, according to Arendt, "has the twofold character of equality and distinction";[62] in other words, "we are all the same, that is, human, in such a way that nobody is ever the same as anyone else who ever lived, lives, or will live."[63]

Each of these aspects of the human condition corresponds to a fundamental human activity; these activities, taken together, make up what Arendt calls the *vita activa*. To life corresponds the human activity of labor, the cyclical and repetitive process of meeting the biological needs of the body and, thus, reproducing and sustaining the conditions necessary for life itself. To worldliness corresponds the activity of work, the process of creating the durable things and artifacts that constitute a common human world. And to plurality corresponds the activity of action, the highest of the three rungs on the ladder of the *vita activa*. Unlike labor and work, action is "the only activity that goes on directly between men without the intermediary of things or matter."[64]

Since action corresponds to the human condition of plurality, it, too, is characterized by both equality and distinction. Through acting and speaking in the public, political realm, the actor is revealed "as a distinct and unique being among equals."[65] Indeed, Arendt gives a compelling argument to demonstrate that this interplay between equality and distinction is inherent in the very nature of action itself:

> If men were not equal, they could neither understand each other and those who came before them nor plan for the future and foresee the needs of those who will come after them. If men were not distinct, . . . they would need neither speech nor action to make themselves understood. Signs and sounds to communicate immediate, identical needs and wants would be enough.[66]

Furthermore, action, as the only activity that goes on between people, is constitutive of the public, political sphere: "The political realm rises directly out of acting together. . . . Thus action not only has the most intimate relationship to the public part of the world common to us all, but is the one activity which constitutes it."[67] Thus, plurality is that aspect of our human condition which corresponds with action, and action is constitutive of the public, political realm.

Plurality, action, and the public realm are related to power in at least two distinct, albeit interconnected, ways. First, "power springs up between men when they act together and vanishes the moment they disperse."[68] That is to say, power is in some sense the result of the collective efforts of actors. Second, power, in turn, provides the condition of possibility for the public realm in which actors come together and pursue the collective projects that give rise to power. As Arendt puts it, "Power preserves the public realm and the space of appearance. . . . Without power, the space of appearance brought forth through action and speech in public will fade away as rapidly as the living deed and the living word."[69] Thus, Arendt contends that power both emerges out of and makes possible collective action among distinct but equal individuals in the public realm.

Power emerges out of collective action, but collective action itself is made possible by the binding force of promising. According to Arendt, the tie that binds people together in political action is "the force of mu-

tual promise or contract."[70] Thus, political collectivities are bound together not by a shared essence or identity but by the promise to work together to attain certain political goals. Arendt's use of the term *contract* as
a synonym for *promise* might be taken to imply that she is assuming a fix-
ity or a permanence to the promises that bind political actors together. If
this is indeed her view of promises, then one might argue that she is
positing a fixed unity to political collectivities that very rarely, if ever, occurs, and that is probably cause for concern if it does. However, the claim
that political actors are bound together by promises, covenants, and con-
tracts does not assume such a fixed unity because Arendt insists that
such agreements are in principle always open to amendment and/or
augmentation. Indeed, Arendt maintains that promises are mere islands
of certainty in a sea of uncertainty, and when they lose this provisional
character they actually "lose their binding power and the whole enter-
prise becomes self-defeating."[71] In other words, promises between political actors that assume a permanent, fixed unity for an indefinite amount
of time cannot possibly be kept, and promises that cannot possibly be
kept of necessity lose their binding force. Thus, the promises that bind us
together as political actors have to be always open to contestation, reinterpretation, and revision.

Moreover, in order to successfully generate power, these promises
must rest on reciprocal and mutual relationships among actors. Hence,
for instance, Arendt praises the key players in the American Revolution
for understanding that "power came into being when and where people
would get together and bind themselves through promises, covenants
and mutual pledges; only such power, which rested on reciprocity and
mutuality, was real power and legitimate."[72] The elements of reciprocity
and mutuality inherent in this conception of power are what give it a
positive normative valence. As Jürgen Habermas puts it, for Arendt,

> power is built up through communicative action; it is a collective effect of
> speech in which reaching agreement is an end in itself for all those in-
> volved.... Arendt regards the development of power as an end in itself. It
> becomes consolidated and embodied in political institutions which secure
> those very forms of life that are centered in reciprocal speech.[73]

Thus, Habermas maintains—contra commentators such as George Kateb
and Martin Jay, who charge Arendt with holding a view of politics that is
completely devoid of normative constraints and considerations—that it
is clear that Arendt's "communications concept of power also has a normative content."[74]

Although I agree with Habermas that Arendt's conception of power
does have a normative core and that she was never guilty of the immoral-

ism or amoralism of which she has been accused, there is nonetheless some merit to Kateb's claim that "the easy response to Arendt's enormous claims for *promise-keeping* is that there is honor among thieves."[75] The problem is not that Arendt ignores the fact that collective immoral actions can easily be seen to count as exercises of power in her positive sense of the term. For instance, in *On Violence*, Arendt acknowledges that

> even the totalitarian ruler, whose chief instrument is torture, needs a power basis. . . . Even the most despotic domination we know of, the rule of master over slaves, who always outnumbered him, did not rest on superior means of coercion as such, but on a superior organization of power—that is, on the organized solidarity of the masters.[76]

Thus, Arendt acknowledges that power, as she understands it, may just as easily emerge out of group interactions that are normatively problematic, or even downright evil, as out of benevolent or peaceful interactions. However, Arendt does not seem to recognize that it is difficult to reconcile this acknowledgment with the normative core of her conception of power. Since she does not recognize this problem, Arendt does not provide a solution for it either. I shall suggest in the next chapter, however, that this problem can be avoided by distinguishing carefully between power understood as the ability to act in concert (what I shall call *power-with*) and the more particular term *solidarity*.

Although Arendt does not seem to realize the full implications of the normative core of her conception of power, this conception nevertheless provides key insights into the theorization of power. I shall argue in the next section that her understanding of power as that which emerges out of and is sustained and nourished by group interactions characterized by reciprocity and mutuality provides the basis for a feminist conception of solidarity; more important, this Arendtian conception of solidarity avoids the problematic essentialism against which Butler's critique of solidarity warns.

Beyond Sisterhood: Rethinking Solidarity

As the identity politics debate has heated up and dragged on, appeals to feminist solidarity have grown increasingly problematic.[77] Early second-wave feminists saw no problem with brandishing the slogan "sisterhood is powerful"; implicit in this slogan is an appeal to the common interests of women, a call for a response to a shared experience (oppression) that binds women together as sisters—hence, to solidarity (at least in one sense of that term). However, by the late 1980s, the critique of any notion of the common interests of women, the common oppression of women, even the category of women per se, was in full swing. This critique rightly pointed out that attempts to specify the essence of women, or even the essence of women's experience of oppression, always held up certain women or the experiences of certain women—most often those women who were "just women," whose identities were "untarnished" by blackness, by queerness, or by membership in the working class—as paradigmatic.[78] In so doing, such attempts marginalized or excluded outright women of color, working-class women, and lesbians. Since the "sisterhood" model of solidarity seems to rely upon these problematic notions of women or of women's common experience, the feminist critique of identity politics necessitates a corresponding critique of solidarity in this sense. It is for reasons such as these that Judith Butler claims that solidarity is "an exclusionary norm . . . that rules out the possibility of a set of actions which disrupt the very borders of identity concepts."[79]

However, as I argued in Chapter 3, Butler's critique of solidarity leads to its own set of problems. This critique is so radical that it has the effect of making it difficult to understand what, if anything, might bind members of the feminist movement together and link that movement to related social struggles against racism and heterosexism; in the wake of the increasing fragmentation of the feminist movement in recent years, this problem seems more and more pressing. The terms of the identity politics debate seem to leave us with only two options, equally unpalatable: Either we embrace the category of women so that we can have some basis for theorizing the common experiences of oppression that bring us together and make collective feminist political action possible, but in so doing, we implicitly marginalize or, worse, exclude legions of women from feminist discourse; or we refuse the category of women altogether, thus avoiding the problem of exclusion, but in so doing, we deny ourselves the ability to theorize the ties that might bind us together to make common cause. But this is a false antithesis; thus, we should not choose either of these options.[80] Instead, our task should be to reformulate the notion of solidarity in such a way that it can account for the power that feminists wield when we act in concert, and yet do so in a way that avoids the problem of exclusion that plagues identity politics. In what follows, I shall argue that Hannah Arendt provides feminists with the resources necessary for reformulating solidarity as a kind of power that emerges out of concerted action—as something that is achieved through action in concert, rather than as the sister-feeling that automatically results from the sharing of a pregiven, fixed, and, hence, repressive, identity. Thus, Arendt helps us to think about how members of oppositional social movements can be united in a way that, far from excluding or repressing difference, embraces and protects it.

Arendt implicitly rejects the notion that group solidarity rests on a shared identity if that identity is understood as resting on an inherent sameness, be it a shared essence, a shared experience of oppression, or what have you. Indeed, for Arendt, sameness cannot be the basis for any political action because the "unitedness of many into one is basically antipolitical; it is the very opposite of the togetherness prevailing in political . . . communities."[81] As discussed above, Arendt maintains that communication and action in concert would be unnecessary, even superfluous, if we were all the same: Everyone would immediately intuit the needs, wants, hopes, and dreams of others because they would be the same as one's own needs, wants, hopes, and dreams. Thus, the very fact that communication and concerted action are necessary in political life indicates the truth of the claim that sameness—and, thus, any notion of identity that is predicated on an appeal to sameness—is antipolitical.

However, the flip side of this is the claim that communication and action in concert would be impossible if we were all radically different. Communication and action in concert depend upon some sort of commonality between individuals; without that commonality, it would be impossible to formulate political goals and to strive to achieve them. Thus, although Arendt rejects the idea that political action can be based on an appeal to sameness, she nonetheless insists that political action cannot be understood at all if one abandons any and all notions of commonality among actors.

In this way, Arendt highlights the dialectical relationship between equality and distinction, commonality and difference. From her standpoint, all action involves this dialectical relationship because it is an unchangeable aspect of the human condition that, as I discussed above, "we are all the same, that is, human, in such a way that nobody is ever the same as anyone else who ever lived, lives, or will live."[82] Thus, for Arendt, action in the political sphere always involves both appearing before our equals and revealing ourselves as unique, distinct persons. For Arendt, action both individuates and establishes relationships; it sets us apart and binds us together. Thus, it seems clear that Arendt would have refused to accept the terms of the identity politics debate, opting instead for an account that stresses the dialectical relationship between identity/nonidentity, commonality/difference, and equality/distinction.[83]

Thus far, I have focused on the dialectical nature of Arendt's general theoretical reflections on the human condition of plurality and on the corresponding activity of action; however, the dialectical tension between commonality and distinction that is at the root of all political life is reflected in a dialectic of identity and nonidentity that can be found in her more explicitly political writings as well. For instance, Arendt's ad-

dress on accepting the Lessing Prize of the Free City of Hamburg illuminates some of the practical political consequences of her theoretical commitments. In that address, Arendt claims that

> the basically simple principle in question here is one that is particularly hard
> to understand in times of defamation and persecution: the principle that *one
> can resist only in terms of the identity that is under attack.* Those who reject such
> identifications on the part of a hostile world may feel wonderfully superior
> to the world, but their superiority is then truly no longer of this world; it is
> the superiority of a more or less well-equipped cloud-cuckoo-land.[54]

The first thing to notice is that these remarks imply that the attempt to
reject all identity categories whatsoever, especially when those identities
are under attack, is profoundly anti-political insofar as it renders all resistance to persecution and domination impossible. To be sure, Arendt's remarks in the Lessing Address are directed not against deconstructive critics of identity but against proponents of humanism who favor
assimilation over a celebration of the unique identity of oppressed and
marginalized groups (or pariah peoples, to put it in Arendtian parlance).
That this group is her target is evident when she says:

> For many years, I considered the only adequate reply to the question, who
> are you? to be: a Jew. That answer alone took into account the reality of per-
> secution. As for the statement with which Nathan the Wise . . . countered the
> command: "Step closer, Jew"—the statement: I am a man—I would have
> considered as nothing but a grotesque and dangerous evasion of reality.[85]

In other words, to appeal to the ideal of humanism and respond "I am a
man (and not just a Jew)" to the command of a persecutor is grotesque in
that it rests on a serious distortion of political realities and dangerous in
that such distortions seriously undermine attempts to resist persecution.
Nevertheless, it seems to me that Arendt's critique applies equally as
well to the deconstructive critique of group identity categories as it does
to the humanistic denial of such categories. After all, in the face of the realities of systematic domination, the claim "I am not a woman—in fact, I
am not even an (identical) I" is no less a grotesque and dangerous denial
of political realities than "I am a human being (not just a woman)."
    Although it seems clear that Arendt would have opposed the kind of
radical deconstruction of identity that rejects any and all appeals to
group identity categories as inherently repressive and exclusionary, her
statement "I am a Jew" also should not be taken to indicate an essentialist
view of Jewish identity. For her, Jewish identity is not predicated on a
shared essence or even on a shared experience of oppression:

> When I use the word "Jew" I do not mean to suggest any special kind of hu-
> man being, . . . [nor do I] refer to a reality burdened or marked out for dis-
> tinction by history. Rather, I was only acknowledging a political fact through
> which my being a member of this group outweighed all other questions of
> personal identity or rather had decided them in favor of anonymity, of
> namelessness.[86]

Thus, Arendt insists that one can affirm in some sense that one is a Jew
without implying that being a Jew involves partaking of some fixed
essence that all Jews share. Affirming membership in an identity group is
a recognition of a political fact: As fact it is undeniable, and to attempt to
deny it is dangerous and deluded; but as political, it is resistible and, ultimately, changeable.

From this example, it seems clear that although Arendt emphasizes
difference, distinction, and uniqueness in her account of politics, she is
unwilling to do so at the expense of any and all invocation of identity categories. Similarly, although she embraces group identities, she is careful
to point out that such categories are not fixed, natural, or even historically determined, but are always knit out of the fabric of difference and
distinction. Sometimes political realities compel us to acknowledge the
political fact of certain identities, identities that are under attack, and, if
we wish to resist, to resist in terms of them. Arendt's refusal to understand Jewish identity in terms of an inherent sameness, a shared essence,
or even a shared history of oppression makes it clear that any conception
of solidarity that one might find in her work would not be predicated on
a repressive and exclusionary conception of identity. This fact—together
with her insistence on acknowledging the political fact of her Jewish
identity, her resolution to resist in terms of that identity when it is under
attack, and her understanding of power as emerging out of collective political action based on reciprocal promises—indicates that her work
might provide an excellent starting point for rethinking the concept of
solidarity.

These various strands of Arendt's thought are woven together in her
discussion in *Eichmann in Jerusalem* of the way that the Danish government and people behaved toward Jews in their country during World
War II; accordingly, this discussion provides a good indication of what a
conception of solidarity inspired by Arendt might look like. Arendt pref-
aces this discussion with the following remark: "One is tempted to rec-
ommend the story as required reading in political science for all students
who wish to learn something about the enormous power potential inherent in non-violent action and in resistance to an opponent possessing
vastly superior means of violence."[87] Indeed, the story of the Danish people's collective resistance to the Nazis is tremendously illuminating for

any discussion of the power that can emerge when individuals act in concert. As Arendt reports it, "When the Germans approached [the Danes] rather cautiously about introducing the yellow badge, they were simply told that the King would be the first to wear it, and the Danish government officials were careful to point out that anti-Jewish measures of any sort would cause their own immediate resignation."[88] Similarly, when the Germans demanded that the Danes turn over the stateless German Jewish refugees who had found asylum in Denmark prior to the war, the Danish government flatly refused: "The Danes . . . explained to the German officials that because the stateless refugees were no longer German citizens, the Nazis could not claim them without Danish assent."[89] Later on, in the fall of 1943, when the Nazis sent police units from Germany to Denmark to round up Jews and ship them off to Theresienstadt, the Danish government warned Jewish officials of the impending roundup, who in turn warned Jews ahead of time to go into hiding; the majority of them were able to go into hiding rather easily "because, in the words of the judgment, 'all sections of the Danish people, from the King down to simple citizens,' stood ready to receive them."[90] Finally, toward the end of the war, wealthy Danish citizens paid for those Jews who could not afford it to cross the water into Sweden, where they were able to receive work permits. This was in marked contrast to the behavior of citizens in most other countries; "even in places where Jews met with genuine sympathy and a sincere willingness to help, they had to pay for it, and the chances poor people had of escaping were nil."[91] All of these events led Eichmann himself to conclude that "for various reasons the actions against the Jews in Denmark has been a failure."[92] Arendt notes that

> politically and psychologically, the most interesting aspect of this incident . . . [is that] it is the only case we know of in which the Nazis met with open native resistance, and the result seems to have been that those exposed to it changed their minds. They themselves apparently no longer looked upon the extermination of a whole people as a matter of course. They had met resistance based on principle, and their "toughness" had melted like butter in the sun.[93]

Arendt's discussion of this case is fascinating on a number of different levels, but for our purposes, three aspects of it seem particularly important. First, the Danish resistance provides one of the most compelling discussions in Arendt's work of a specific example of the kind of collective power that can emerge out of action in concert.[94] Second, it is interesting to note that Arendt presents the fact that many Danes hid Jews in their homes and many more were willing to do so not as a private but as a *political* act, one that contributes to the collective political power that the

Danes were able to exercise in resistance to the Nazis. This characterization lends support to the attitudinal distinction among the public, the
private, and the social that I discussed above, since Arendt's account indicates that these acts were political not because of the realm in which
they took place but because they were oriented toward the common
good. The example of the Danish resistance thus provides further evidence that Arendt's conception of power can be stripped of some of its
metaphysical baggage and put to work in a discussion of feminist issues,
even those that challenge the traditional public/private dichotomy. Finally, Arendt makes it clear that the Danish people resisted in terms of
the Jewish identity that was under attack: When the Nazis approached
them about distributing the yellow star, the king of Denmark vowed to
be the first to wear it, even though he himself was not a Jew. Thus, it is
possible to resist *in terms of* the identity that is under attack without being
a member of the group whose identity is under attack. One does not need
to "be" a Jew to resist in terms of a Jewish identity under attack. Thus,
Arendt's view is that collective political movements are held together not
by a shared identity but by the mutual promises of distinct individuals to
work together for the attainment of a common political goal.

Arendt's discussion of the Danish resistance to the Nazis offers crucial
insights into the development of a feminist conception of solidarity that
can be acceptable in light of the lessons we have learned from the identity politics debate. Drawing on Arendt, we can view solidarity as the collective power that grows out of action in concert, binds members of the
feminist movement together, and enables feminists to build coalitions
with other oppositional social movements. This conception avoids the
problems that plague the sisterhood model of solidarity because it is not
predicated on an exclusionary and repressive conception of women's
shared essence or experience of oppression. Instead, the feminist conception of solidarity that we can cull from Arendt's work rests on a mediated
conception of group identity. The category of women is neither incontrovertible fact nor pure fiction; it is a political fact; as fact it is undeniable,
and to attempt to deny it is to blind oneself to political realities, but as political it is changeable. One changes it by resisting, but one can resist only
in terms of the political fact of an identity under attack. However, as
Arendt's discussion of the Danes makes clear, one need not "be" a
woman to join in the collective effort to resist women's subordination. A
consideration of Arendt's work thus prompts a shift from thinking of solidarity among women as the power of sisterhood to thinking of solidarity among feminists (women and men) as the power of those who pledge
to work together to fight relations of subordination. As Mary Dietz puts
it, Arendt makes possible a "politics of shared differences."[95] The conception that goes along with such a politics views solidarity as something

that is achieved through a mutual promise or shared commitment to act in concert, not an exclusionary unity that is presumed in advance. And although this power grows out of promises and shared commitments, these commitments must be subject to contestation and revision; otherwise, the promises will cease to bind and the power will disappear. Thus, this conception offers feminists a way of understanding the requirements for forging relations of solidarity between unique, distinct women (and men) of different races, classes, ethnicities, and sexual orientations, who are, as a result of their differences, differently empowered.

A Limitation to Arendt's Conception of Power

Despite the insights into solidarity that can be gleaned from Arendt's political theory, a significant limitation in her conception of power remains. Since Arendt explicitly excludes from her definition of power any negative sense of power, such as constraining the options of others or getting others to do what one wants, it fails to account for the kinds of domination relations that a feminist conception of power must be able to illuminate. Arendt paints a rather rosy picture of power relations that, although quite useful for theorizing the positive collective empowerment of political actors, is singularly unhelpful for theorizing the systemic relations of domination against which such actors struggle.

One might object to this line of argument by suggesting that, although Arendt screened such negative elements out of her conception of power, she nevertheless provided a model for conceptualizing them in her discussions of violence, authority, and strength. Thus, one might suggest, it is not the case that Arendt fails to conceptualize power understood as domination; she simply uses different terms to describe these kinds of relationships. If this were the case, then one might suggest that her conceptions of violence, authority, and strength could provide insight into the kinds of domination relationships that feminists are struggling to transform and/or overturn.

However, violence, authority, and strength, as Arendt defines these terms, are not adequate to make sense of the kinds of domination relations in which feminists are interested. Let us examine violence first. Violence may aptly describe the power that states potentially have over their citizens or over each other, but it is less helpful for illuminating the kind of power that men exercise over women. For instance, a husband may exercise power over his wife by using implements of violence such as his penis, in unwanted intercourse, and/or his fists, or even his access to weapons as instruments of coercion. However, masculine dominance is not necessarily manifested in this way. Typically, insofar as husbands exercise power over their wives, they do so through more subtle personal and impersonal structural and institutional mechanisms and relations, such as the gender division of paid and unpaid labor. In other words, the power that husbands exercise over their wives goes beyond the parameters of Arendt's conception of violence. Because violence corresponds to only one aspect of male power, it is not adequate to illuminate all the kinds of domination in which feminists are interested.

Similarly, authority proves too thin a concept to capture the kind of power that men can exercise over women. For example, in contemporary postindustrial societies, in which the influence of traditional religions has steadily declined, the authority of the husband or father has, to some extent, broken down. Many women no longer obey their husband unquestioningly, simply by virtue of their respect for his position or person. However, despite the fact that wives no longer uniformly grant power to their husbands in view of his unquestioned superiority, husbands remain in positions of power over their wives. Their power is just mediated through more complex cultural, institutional, and structural forms.

Finally, strength also fails to capture the full range of power that men can exercise over women. Male power over women is not a function of an inherent property or characteristic; on the contrary, it is the result of a set of social and, hence, mutable relations. Thus, to return to our example, husbands are able to abuse their wives not because of an inherent, physical property such as greater physical prowess, although in some cases such a property will exacerbate the abuse; rather, husbands are able to abuse their wives because their position in the social and institutional network permits and, to a certain extent, encourages them to do so.

Thus, the concepts that Arendt employs for discussing instances of coercion or domination are insufficient for explaining the power that men exercise over women. My criticism of Arendt on this point is related to a point made by Habermas, who takes Arendt to task on the grounds that her conception of power unnecessarily "screens all strategic elements, as force, out of politics."[96] To ignore the strategic dimension of politics, according to Habermas, is simply to deny the political realities of modern societies. Although he credits Arendt with recognizing that "strategic contests for political power neither call forth nor maintain those institutions in which that power is anchored," Habermas nevertheless maintains that "we cannot exclude the element of strategic action from the concept of the political."[97] In other words, Habermas also maintains that Arendt's conception paints too rosy a picture of power and, as a result, is unable to illuminate a number of the social phenomena that we seek to target when we talk about power.

Although I agree with Habermas that Arendt's conception of power as action in concert does not cover strategic uses and abuses of power, I would emphasize that it is not the case that this conception precludes an analysis of such aspects of power. As Maurizio Passerin d'Entreves puts it,

> [Arendt] was not unaware of the strategic competition for political power; her point, rather, was to show that political institutions had to rest on the consent of the people, that their legitimacy derived from the power of common conviction attained through a process of unconstrained deliberation. ... [P]olitical institutions may indeed be the locus of a strategic competition for power, but they are legitimate only so long as structures of undistorted communication find their expression in them.[98]

That Arendt was not unaware of the strategic competition for political power is evident, for instance, in *The Origins of Totalitarianism*, in which she talks about power in very conventional terms as strategic action and cites Hobbes as the theorist of power *par excellence*.[99] To be sure, the conception of power developed in *The Human Condition* does not illuminate strategic power relations, nor does it account for instances of domination. However, to my mind, these criticisms merely point out the need for integrating Arendt's account of power with an account that does target such strategic domination relations. Thus, such criticisms lend support to my attempt to integrate Arendt's account of power with that of Foucault and Butler, since their attention to the strategic and sinister exercise of power can be understood as correcting for the lack of this dimension in her view, just as her communicative conception of power corrects for the lack of crucial normative distinctions in theirs.

With respect to this kind of integrative approach to a feminist conception power, Arendt provides a final crucial insight. Although, as I discussed at some length above, she spends a great deal of time and care distinguishing power from violence, authority, and strength, she recognizes that it is common for more than one (and perhaps even all) of these phenomena to be present in the same situation. Thus, she notes that "these distinctions, though by no means arbitrary, hardly ever correspond to watertight compartments in the real world. . . . From this it does not follow that authority, power, and violence are all the same."[100] This observation shall prove pivotal for my task in Chapter 5 of delineating the different senses of the term *power* in which feminists are interested. In that chapter, using the analyses of power provided by Foucault, Butler, and Arendt as a springboard, I shall attempt to draw analytical distinctions between the various ways of exercising power that are relevant for a feminist conception; however, in so doing, I shall bear in mind Arendt's reminder that when we examine real institutions and practices, we are likely to find all of these modalities of power present in one and the same situation or relationship.

Notes

1. For some examples of the recent literature, see Seyla Benhabib, *The Reluctant Modernism of Hannah Arendt* (London: Sage, 1996); Lisa Disch, *Hannah Arendt and the Limits of Philosophy* (Ithaca: Cornell University Press, 1994); Bonnie Honig, ed., *Feminist Interpretations of Hannah Arendt* (University Park: Pennsylvania State Press, 1995); and the last three essays in Larry May and Jerome Kohn, eds., *Hannah Arendt: Twenty Years Later* (Cambridge, Mass.: MIT Press, 1996).

2. For Arendt's discussion of the black student movement, see *On Violence* (New York: Harcourt, Brace, and Co., 1969), p. 44; for her argument against federally enforced desegregation, see "Reflections on Little Rock," *Dissent* 6 (Winter 1959): 45–56. For an insightful commentary on this essay, see James Bohman, "The Moral Costs of Political Pluralism: The Dilemmas of Difference and Equality in Arendt's 'Reflections on Little Rock,'" in May and Kohn, eds., *Hannah Arendt: Twenty Years Later*.

3. But see Morris Kaplan, "Refiguring the Jewish Question: Arendt, Proust, and the Politics of Sexuality," in Honig, ed., *Feminist Interpretations of Hannah Arendt*, for an attempt to tease out an Arendtian politics of sexuality.

4. For attempts to do the former, see Wendy Brown, *Manhood and Politics* (Totowa, N.J.: Rowman and Littlefield, 1988); Anne Norton, "Heart of Darkness," in Honig, ed., *Feminist Interpretations of Hannah Arendt*; Mary O'Brien, *The Politics of Reproduction* (Boston: Routledge and Kegan Paul, 1981); and Adrienne Rich, "Conditions for Work: The Common World of Women," in *On Lies, Secrets, and Silence: Selected Prose 1966–1978* (New York: W. W. Norton and Co., 1979). For attempts to do the latter, see Jean Bethke Elshstain, *Meditations on Modern Political Thought: Masculine/Feminine Themes from Luther to Arendt* (New York: Praeger, 1986); and Nancy Hartsock, *Money, Sex, and Power*, ch. 9.

5. Judith Butler, *Excitable Speech* (New York: Routledge, 1997), p. 179, note 9.

6. Hannah Arendt, *On Revolution* (New York: Penguin, 1990), p. 19. See also Arendt, *The Human Condition* (Chicago: University of Chicago Press, 1958), pp. 25–27.

7. Dana Villa and Bonnie Honig have recently drawn more attention to the Nietzschean and Heideggerian elements of Arendt's thought and have interpreted Arendt as a nascent postmodernist. See Honig, "Toward an Agonistic Feminism: Hannah Arendt and the Politics of Identity," in Judith Butler and Joan W. Scott, eds., *Feminists Theorize the Political* (New York: Routledge, 1992); and Villa, *Arendt and Heidegger: The Fate of the Political* (Princeton: Princeton University Press, 1996).

8. Nietzsche's influence on Foucault is reflected throughout his work, both in his philosophical methodology and in his choice of topics of study, and is specifically addressed by Foucault in "Nietzsche, Genealogy, History," in Michel Foucault, *Language, Counter-Memory, Practice*, ed. Donald F. Bouchard (Ithaca: Cornell University Press, 1977), pp. 139–164. Indeed, given the clear Nietzschean influence on Foucault's thought, it might be surprising that he once made the following statement: "My entire philosophical development was determined by my reading of Heidegger" (see Foucault, "The Return of Morality," in Lawrence D. Kritzman, ed., *Michel Foucault: Politics, Philosophy, Culture* (New York: Routledge, 1988), p. 250).

9. Benhabib, *The Reluctant Modernism of Hannah Arendt*, pp. 197–198.

10. Michel Foucault, *The Order of Things: An Archaeology of the Human Sciences* (New York: Vintage, 1973). But see also Foucault, "On Power," in Kritzman, ed., *Michel Foucault: Politics, Philosophy, Culture*, pp. 99–100, where he argues that this reading of *The Order of Things* is wrong. He claims that his goal in *The Order of Things* was that of "posing discontinuity as a problem and above all as a problem to be resolved" (p. 100). However, it is difficult to see how this reading can be reconciled with the methodological claims that Foucault makes about discontinuity in historical analysis in the Introduction to *The Archaeology of Knowledge*.

11. Michel Foucault, *The Archaeology of Knowledge and the Discourse on Language*, trans. A. M. Sheridan Smith (New York: Pantheon, 1972), pp. 15–16.

12. Judith Butler, *Subjects of Desire: Hegelian Reflections in Twentieth Century France* (New York: Columbia University Press, 1987), p. 180.

13. Arendt, *On Violence*, p. 28.

14. Ibid.

15. Benhabib, *The Reluctant Modernism of Hannah Arendt*, p. 88.

16. See Arendt, *The Human Condition*, pp. 8–9; and on the connection between natality and revolution, see Arendt, *On Revolution*, passim.

17. Arendt, *On Violence*, p. 28, quoting G.W.F. Hegel, *Vorlesungen uber die Geschichte der Philosophie*, ed. Johannes Hoffmeister (Leipzig, 1938), p. 100.

18. On this point, see also Morris Kaplan, *Sexual Justice: Democratic Citizenship and the Politics of Desire* (New York: Routledge, 1997), p. 156.

19. Arendt, *The Human Condition*, p. 40.

20. Seyla Benhabib correctly points out, however, that "Arendt presupposes that such normalizations occur without explicating the social mechanisms of the exercise of power, or the microphysics of power, which make such normalization possible" (see Benhabib, *The Reluctant Modernism of Hannah Arendt*, p. 26).

21. Michel Foucault, "On the Genealogy of Ethics: An Overview of Work in Progress," in Paul Rabinow, ed., *The Foucault Reader* (New York: Pantheon, 1984), p. 341.

22. See Hannah Arendt, *Lectures on Kant's Political Philosophy* (Chicago: University of Chicago Press, 1982).

23. Arendt, *The Human Condition*, p. 188.

24. Arendt, "The Crisis in Culture," in *Between Past and Future* (New York: Penguin, 1954), pp. 218, 219, 220.

25. Given this similarity, it is not surprising that both Foucault and Arendt have been criticized for an "aestheticization of politics" and grouped with such "young conservative" anti-modernists as Heidegger, Ernst Jünger, and Carl Schmitt. For this charge against Foucault, see Jürgen Habermas, "Modernity Versus Post-Modernity," *New German Critique* 22 (Winter 1981): 3–14. For this charge against Arendt, see Martin Jay, "Hannah Arendt: Opposing Views," *Partisan Review* 45:3 (Summer 1978): 348–368. For a critical assessment of this charge against Foucault, see Nancy Fraser, "Michel Foucault: A 'Young Conservative'?" in Fraser, *Unruly Practices: Power, Gender, and Discourse in Contemporary Critical Theory* (Minneapolis: University of Minnesota Press, 1989). And for a defense of Arendt against Jay's critique, see Maurizio Passerin d'Entreves, *The Political Philosophy of Hannah Arendt* (New York: Routledge, 1994), pp. 85–95.

26. Arendt, *On Violence*, p. 13.

27. Arendt, *The Human Condition*, p. 184; emphasis added.

28. Honig, "Toward an Agonistic Feminism," p. 232.

29. On this point, see Kaplan, *Sexual Justice*, p. 154.

30. Arendt, *The Human Condition*, p. 222.

31. Ibid., p. 220.

32. See ibid.

33. Michel Foucault, *The History of Sexuality, Vol. 1: An Introduction*, trans. Robert Hurley (New York: Vintage, 1978), p. 94.

34. Arendt, *The Human Condition*, p. 200. See also Arendt, *On Violence*, p. 44.

35. Benhabib, *The Reluctant Modernism of Hannah Arendt*, pp. 138–139.

36. Ibid., p. 142.

37. For instance, Arendt argues that the violent excesses of the French Revolution were the result of the attempt to address private concerns with public political means. (See Arendt, *On Revolution*, passim.)

38. Arendt, *The Human Condition*, p. 45.

39. Benhabib, *The Reluctant Modernism of Hannah Arendt*, p. 140.

40. Ibid., p. 141.

41. Cf. Hanna Fenichel Pitkin, "Justice: On Relating Private and Public," *Political Theory* 9:3 (August 1981): 342.

42. Arendt, *The Human Condition*, p. 46; emphasis added. Quoted in Benhabib, *The Reluctant Modernism of Hannah Arendt*, p. 139.

43. Ibid., p. 216. Quoted in Benhabib, *The Reluctant Modernism of Hannah Arendt*, p. 142.

44. Benhabib, *The Reluctant Modernism of Hannah Arendt*, p. 145.

45. For a discussion of this point, see ibid., pp. 146–155.

46. This is the strategy employed by Nancy Fraser, who sees the rise of the social as a positive development insofar as it has facilitated the public contestation and resignification of needs. (See Fraser, "Women, Welfare, and the Politics of Need Interpretation," in Fraser, *Unruly Practices*, p. 160, note 32.)

47. Elizabeth Young-Bruehl, *Hannah Arendt: For Love of the World* (New Haven: Yale University Press, 1982), p. 238. Quoted in Mary Dietz, "Feminist Receptions of Hannah Arendt," in Honig, ed., *Feminist Interpretations of Hannah Arendt*, p. 19.

48. Arendt, *The Human Condition*, p. 176.

49. See Arendt, *On Violence*, p. 46.

50. Ibid., p. 42.

51. See ibid., p. 51.

52. Ibid.

53. Ibid., p. 80.

54. Ibid., p. 56.

55. Ibid., p. 45.

56. See ibid., p. 44.

57. Ibid.

58. Arendt, *On Revolution*, p. 175.

59. Arendt, *On Violence*, p. 44.

60. Ibid.

61. Arendt, *The Human Condition*, p. 7.

62. Ibid., p. 175.

63. Ibid., p. 8.

64. Ibid., p. 7.

65. Ibid., p. 178.

66. Ibid., pp. 175–176.

67. Ibid., p. 198.

68. Ibid., p. 200.

69. Ibid., p. 204.

70. Ibid., pp. 245.

71. Ibid., p. 244.

72. Arendt, *On Revolution*, p. 181.

73. Jürgen Habermas, "Hannah Arendt's Communications Concept of Power," in Lewis P. Hinchman and Sandra K. Hinchman, eds., *Hannah Arendt: Critical Essays* (Albany: SUNY Press, 1994), pp. 213–214.

74. Ibid., p. 214. Cf. George Kateb, *Hannah Arendt: Politics, Conscience, Evil* (Totowa, N.J.: Rowman and Allanheld, 1984), pp. 28–44; and Jay, "Hannah Arendt: Opposing Views," p. 353.

75. Kateb, *Hannah Arendt: Politics, Conscience, Evil*, p. 35; emphasis Kateb's.

76. Arendt, *On Violence*, p. 50.

77. For a recent attempt to rethink the concept of solidarity from a feminist perspective, see Jodi Dean, *Solidarity of Strangers: Feminism After Identity Politics* (Berkeley: University of California Press, 1996).

78. For an excellent discussion of this point, see Elizabeth Spelman, *Inessential Woman: Problems of Exclusion in Feminist Thought* (Boston: Beacon, 1988).

79. Judith Butler, *Gender Trouble* (New York: Routledge, 1990), p. 15.

80. For an excellent argument to this effect, see Allison Weir, *Sacrificial Logics* (New York: Routledge, 1996).

81. Arendt, *The Human Condition*, p. 214.

82. Ibid., p. 8.

83. By emphasizing the dialectical nature of Arendt's account, I am going against the trend in recent feminist assessments of Arendt to read her as a deconstructive critic of identity. For examples of this kind of reading, see Honig, "Toward an Agonistic Feminism"; Joanne Cutting-Gray, "Hannah Arendt, Feminism, and the Politics of Alterity: 'What Will We Lose If We Win?'" *Hypatia* 8:1 (Winter 1993): 37; and Lisa Disch, "On Friendship in 'Dark Times,'" in Honig, ed., *Feminist Interpretations of Hannah Arendt*. I discuss these interpretations in more detail in "Solidarity After Identity Politics: Hannah Arendt and the Power of Feminist Theory," forthcoming in *Philosophy and Social Criticism*.

84. Hannah Arendt, "On Humanity in Dark Times: Thoughts About Lessing," in *Men in Dark Times* (New York: Harcourt, Brace, and World, 1968), p. 18; emphasis added.

85. Ibid., pp. 17–18.

86. Ibid., p. 18.

87. Hannah Arendt, *Eichmann in Jerusalem: A Report of the Banality of Evil* (New York: Penguin, 1963), p. 171.

88. Ibid.

89. Ibid., p. 172.

90. Ibid., p. 174.

91. Ibid.

92. Ibid.

93. Ibid., p. 175.

94. For a more contemporary example of the usefulness of Arendt's conception of power, see Vaclav Havel, "The Power of the Powerless" in Havel et al., *The Power of the Powerless: Citizens Against the State in Central-Eastern Europe* (New York: ME Sharpe, Inc., 1985).

95. Mary Dietz, "Hannah Arendt and Feminist Politics," in Hinchman and Hinchman, eds., *Hannah Arendt: Critical Essays*, p. 236.

96. Habermas, "Hannah Arendt's Communications Concept of Power," p. 220.

97. Ibid., p. 222.

98. Passerin d'Entreves, *The Political Philosophy of Hannah Arendt*, p. 100.

99. See Hannah Arendt, *The Origins of Totalitarianism* (New York: Harcourt, Brace, and Co., 1973), pp. 135–147. On this point, see also Margaret Canovan, *Hannah Arendt: A Reinterpretation of Her Political Thought* (Cambridge, Eng.: Cambridge University Press, 1992), p. 208.

100. Arendt, *On Violence*, p. 46.

5

A Feminist Conception
of Power

Each of the theorists whom we have considered up to this point offers a distinct set of contributions to a feminist conception of power. Foucault's genealogy of power provides a compelling alternative to juridical accounts that assume that power is fundamentally repressive, that it always functions by saying no. By contrast, Foucault claims that power is inherently productive, and that its productive and repressive aspects are complexly intertwined; thus, power produces by repressing and represses by producing. Because one of the key effects of power is the subject, this dialectic of production and repression is also evident in Foucault's account of subjection: One is both subject to power and at the same time able to take up the position of a subject in and through power. Thus, Foucault's account of power offers an insight that is lacking in many of the feminist discussions of power that I discussed in Chapter 1: namely, that the domination and the empowerment of an individual are complexly intertwined. However, despite the brilliance of Foucault's conceptual insight into the functioning of power, his analysis is plagued by a series of problems. He fails to make normative distinctions between different uses of power and, as a result, ends up painting power as the night in which all cows are black; he neglects to make good on his aim of integrating a genealogical analysis of power with a genealogy of resistance; and he views power in solely strategic terms, the result of which is a blindness to relations of solidarity. But, from a conceptual standpoint, the most serious problem of all is the paradox of agency that emerges out of his analysis of subjection: If we are always subjects in the sense of being subjected to myriad repressive power relations, then in what sense can we be said to have the capacity to act at all? And, on the flip side, if we are always subjects in the sense of having the capacity to act, then in what sense can we be said to be constrained by social forces?

Judith Butler's Foucaultian-feminist conception of power offers a solution to this conceptual problem. By integrating the Derridean notion of citationality or iterability into the Foucaultian account of subjection, Butler offers an account of what it is that mediates between the two poles of subjection. In this way, Butler resolves the Foucaultian paradox of agency. In her view, subjects are compelled to cite the sex/gender norms that constrain them. Since the norms must be cited by subjects in order to be reproduced, it cannot be the case that we are completely determined by them; but since we are compelled to cite the norms in some way or another, neither are we completely unconstrained by social forces. However, Butler's analysis has its own limitations. On the one hand, unlike Foucault, Butler focuses too narrowly on the discursive as the dimension through which power is exercised and reproduced; thus, she subsumes all aspects of social and cultural life under the umbrella of discourse. On the other hand, like Foucault, Butler explicitly avoids making the kinds of normative distinctions between harmful and beneficial uses of power; and, also like Foucault, she seems to presume a strategic conception of power that renders her analysis blind to relations of solidarity.

By contrast, Hannah Arendt conceives of power fundamentally in communicative rather than strategic terms; thus, her conception provides an excellent starting point for a reexamination of solidarity. In this way, Arendt's analysis of power addresses a major conceptual lacuna of the analyses of Foucault and Butler. Further, the analysis of solidarity that can be gleaned from Arendt's work escapes Butler's criticism that solidarity is an exclusionary norm predicated on a problematic sameness or identity. However, Arendt's analysis falls prey to limitations precisely the opposite of those encountered by Foucault and Butler. First, whereas Foucault and Butler fail to provide a sufficient normative framework for their analyses of power and, thus, fall into normative confusions, the core of Arendt's conception of power is the normative ideal of reciprocity or mutuality. However, Arendt fails to reconcile this normative core with her admission of the fact that power might emerge out of group interactions that are normatively problematic. Thus, Arendt tends to paint too rosy a picture of power; in so doing, she falls into a different sort of normative confusion. In other words, whereas Foucault's and Butler's analyses of power suffer because of their presupposition that power is always and only strategic, Arendt's analysis suffers from the opposite presupposition—the assumption that power is always and only communicative. This leads to the second limitation of Arendt's analysis of power: Whereas Arendt's conception is quite useful for theorizing the positive collective empowerment of feminist actors, it is less helpful for theorizing the systemic relations of domination against which such actors struggle.

In this concluding chapter, I offer a conception of power that attempts to weave together the insights of these three theorists, while avoiding the pitfalls and lacunae of their respective analyses. Drawing on the insights into power gleaned from my analyses of Foucault, Butler, and Arendt, I introduce a conception of power that can illuminate domination, resistance, and solidarity and that highlights the complex ways in which they are interrelated. Drawing on Foucault and Butler, my account emphasizes the dialectical relationships between subjects who are endowed with the capacity to act and the discursive and nondiscursive forces to which they are subjected. Furthermore, drawing on Arendt, this account emphasizes the mutual and reciprocal interactions among subjects (in the dual sense of the term). Moreover, in order to avoid the normative confusions that plague Foucault, Butler, and Arendt, I reject the presupposition that power is either inherently strategic (and thus normatively suspect) or inherently communicative (and thus normatively beneficial); instead, I offer normative distinctions between different modalities of power.

In what follows, I begin by considering in detail the kinds of interests that feminists bring to the study of power. From these interests, I derive the definitions of some key "power terms,"[1] definitions that I then situate vis-à-vis other influential conceptions of power. In the final section, I offer some methodological considerations for how best to go about studying power as I have defined it. These methodological exhortations take the form of a series of analytic perspectives from which power should be viewed.

Defining Power

Myriad different, and in many cases contradictory, definitions of power are influential in contemporary social and political theory. In fact, the lack of agreement amongst social and political theorists about how to define power has led some to abandon the hope of arriving at a widely accepted definition. As Steven Lukes puts the point: "It is more likely that the very search for such a definition is a mistake. For the variations in what interests us when we are interested in power run deep . . . , and what unites the various views of power is too thin and formal to provide a generally satisfying definition, applicable to all cases."[2] In light of this serious and ongoing debate, I must emphasize at the outset that I am not attempting to offer a "generally satisfying definition" of power that will be "applicable to all cases." Rather, my aim is to offer an analysis of power that will prove useful for feminist theorists who seek to comprehend, critique, and contest the subordination of women.[3]

With that in mind, let us return to the question that I posed in the Introduction: "What interests feminists when we are interested in power?"

Feminists bring at least three particular interests to a study of power. The first and perhaps the most striking is our interest in understanding the ways men dominate women, an interest that remains the impetus of much feminist research. Furthermore, the exposure in recent years of the racial and class bias of much of feminist theory has signaled the need for feminists to think seriously about how some women dominate others on the basis of their race, class, ethnicity, age, or sexual orientation.[4] A feminist conception of power thus needs to be able to illuminate a complex and interrelated array of systems of domination—an array including sexism, racism, heterosexism, and class oppression, to name only the most conspicuous dimensions. These related concerns require an adequate feminist analysis of power to shed light on the concept of domination more generally.

However, as noted by some of the feminists reviewed in Chapter 1, a discussion of domination will not satisfy all the interests that feminists have in studying power. As I argued in that chapter, to think of power solely in terms of domination leads one to neglect the power that women do have. This neglect, in turn, leads some feminists not only to underemphasize the ways that some women are in positions of dominance over others but also to overemphasize the ways that women are victimized. The recognition of these inadequacies gives rise to a second feminist concern with power: our interest in understanding the power that women do have—that is, empowerment.

This need to theorize the power that women retain in spite of masculine domination often manifests itself in a concern with a specific use to which empowerment can be put—namely, resistance. If the interest in empowerment corresponds to the concern with the power that women exercise in spite of male domination, then the interest in resistance corresponds to feminists' concern with the power that women can wield to oppose male domination. In other words, whereas the feminist interest in empowerment arises out of the need to theorize the power that women have *in spite of* the power that men exercise over us, the interest in resistance emerges out of the need to understand the power that women exercise specifically *as a response to* such domination.

The third interest that feminist theorists bring to the discussion of power comes in the wake of charges that the mainstream feminist movement has marginalized women of color, lesbians, and working-class women. In response to this charge, feminists must be able to think about the kind of power that a diverse group of women can exercise collectively when we work together to define, and strive to achieve, feminist aims. That is, we have an interest in theorizing the kind of collective power that can bridge the diversity of individuals who make up the feminist movement. This interest in collective power also arises out of our need to understand how feminists can build coalitions with other social movements, such as the racial equality movement, the gay rights movement, and/or new labor movements. In short, we need a theory of power that can conceptualize solidarity. Moreover, not just any conception of solidarity will do; we shall have to formulate our conception in such a way that it is able to avoid the charge that solidarity is an exclusionary and repressive concept that is always predicated on some inherent sameness or identity.

In sum, then, a feminist conception of power must be able to make sense of masculine domination, feminine empowerment and resistance, and feminist solidarity and coalition-building. Yet these different sorts of power relations do not all fall under the same sense of the general term *power*. Rather, each of them represents a particular way of exercising power. Our interest in domination is in the particular kinds of power that men are able to exercise *over* women. Our interest in empowerment and resistance is in the power that women have *to* act in spite of or as a response to such domination. Our interest in solidarity and coalition-building is in the power that feminists exercise *with* each other and with men in allied social movements. Feminists' diverse interests in the study of power thus give rise to three basic senses of *power* that our conception will have to illuminate: power-over, power-to, and power-with. Before we can arrive at a conception that will allow us to think of domination, empowerment/resistance, and solidarity/coalition-building together as instances of power—and, more important, that will allow us to analyze these instances in their interrelatedness—we must first consider each of these different senses of the term *power* in itself.

Power-Over

I shall define *power-over* as the ability of an actor or set of actors to constrain the choices available to another actor or set of actors in a nontrivial way. This definition is similar to Thomas Wartenberg's definition of power-over: "A social agent A has *power over* another social agent B if and only if A strategically constrains B's action-environment."[5] I have omitted *strategically* from my definition of power-over because it seems to imply that those who have power over others have that power intentionally.[6] The difficulty with an account that sees power-over as the result of an actor's strategy or intentions is that it ignores the ways one can, as Lukes puts it, "have or exercise power without deliberately seeking to do so, in routine or unconsidered ways, without grasping the effects [one] can or do[es] bring about."[7] It strikes me as particularly important for feminists to define power-over without reference to strategies or intentions because much of the power that men exercise over women is exercised "in routine or unconsidered ways" by men who do not deliberately intend to do so. Indeed, not only is power over women exercised by men who do not deliberately intend to do so, but I would argue that it is even exercised by men who deliberately intend *not* to do so. This is so because, whatever their intentions, these men are still acting within a set of cultural, institutional, and structural relations of power that work to the advantage of dominant groups and to the disadvantage of women and other subordinated groups.[8]

One aspect of my definition of power-over needs clarification—namely, the phrase "in a nontrivial way." In some cases, an agent constrains the choices of another in ways that we would hesitate to call exercises of power at all. If two people each have a craving for chocolate, and one eats the last brownie in the house, then she has constrained the other's options for fulfilling his or her chocolate craving. In a broad spectrum of cases, this constraint seems too trivial to consider an instance of power-over. However, if one who eats the brownie is well-fed and the other is severely malnourished, then this action could well be viewed as an exercise of power-over. There is no general rule here; the claim that an actor or set of actors exercises power over another or others will depend to some extent on the context.

Before I go on to define *domination* and consider its relation to the more general sense of power-over, let me situate my definition with respect to other ways of conceptualizing power-over. First, my definition is broad enough to include both decisions and nondecisions.[9] An actor may constrain the choices of another either by making a direct decision that he or she will have to accommodate or by intentionally or unintentionally maintaining a course of action that limits the set of options from which he or she will be able to choose. Second, this definition covers both overt behavior and anticipated reactions: An actor's options can be constrained both by the overt behavior of another and by his or her anticipation of the other's negative reaction to some subset of his or her options.[10] Third, because it makes no mention of the articulated interests of either party, this definition can account for power-over relations that disadvantage actors with respect to both their avowed interests and those interests we believe them to have that they do not avow.[11] Finally, by conceptualizing power-over as a constraint on an actor's or set of actors' options, this definition avoids conceiving of power solely on a dyadic or interventional model.[12] In other words, this definition allows us to theorize both the power that actors wield in particular relationships and the power that such actors wield by virtue of the cultural, social, institutional, and structural relations within which each of their particular relationships takes shape. Thus, this definition accords with the basic insight—shared by Foucault, Butler, and Arendt—that power is fundamentally relational.

Although domination represents one way of exercising power over others, the terms *domination* and *power-over* cannot be simply synonymous. We can easily think of situations in which one agent constrains the choices available to others in a nontrivial way that we would hesitate to call instances of domination. For example, a basketball coach exercises a certain amount of power over her players: She has the ability to constrain their options as basketball players in nontrivial ways by deciding what will happen at practice, who will play which position, who will start the game, and so on. However, we would hesitate to say that being a coach necessarily involves dominating one's players, although some coaches may use their position in this way. On the contrary, coaches are there to help their players develop new skills, increase their confidence, and, if all goes well, experience the pleasure of victory in competition.[13] Each of these goals points to a use of power-over others that is not harmful, and that does not seem to capture what feminists mean by domination. Therefore, *power-over* must be a broader concept than *domination*. Furthermore, this example indicates that the former can be distinguished from the latter by means of a normative criterion: Coaching is not an instance of domination because the power the coach has over her players is exercised for their benefit, rather than for their disadvantage. Thus, we might define *domination* with reference to a normative criterion as well: Domination entails the ability of an actor or set of actors to constrain the choices of another actor or set of actors in a nontrivial way and in a way that works to the others' disadvantage.[14] Domination thus turns out to be a particular application of power understood as power-over.

Power-To

However, power-over is not the only sense of power that our conception needs to be able to illuminate.[15] After all, resistance and empowerment cannot be understood best as instances of power-over. Rather, these terms seem to describe the capacity of an agent to act in spite of or in response to the power wielded over her by others. As I discussed in Chapter 1, most feminists who view power in terms of empowerment consider this conception of power explicitly to contradict the masculinist definition of power as a dominating and controlling power over others.[16] Nor is the notion of resistance fully illuminated by power-over as defined here; although particular instances of resistance may take the form of placing constraints on the options of the would-be aggressor, resistance seems fundamentally to involve asserting one's capacity to act in the face of the domination of another agent.

If we understand empowerment and resistance in this way, then we can see that they are not completely captured by the term *power-over*. The feminist interest in empowerment and resistance accordingly requires that we understand power in a second sense: the sense of power-to. I define *power-to* as the ability of an individual actor to attain an end or series of ends.[17] This way of defining power-to suggests that the terms *empowerment* and *power-to* are roughly synonymous. Feminists are interested in empowerment because we are interested in how members of subordinated groups retain the power to act despite their subordination—more particularly, in our ability to attain certain ends in spite of the subordination of women. This is an interest in power understood as power-to.

However, *power-to* or *empowerment* cannot be considered equivalent to *resistance*. Just as I can assert my power-to act as a response to a system of domination, I can conceivably assert my power-to act by dominating others.[18] Thus, in the same way that domination represents a particular way of exercising power-over, resistance seems to represent a particular way of exercising power-to or empowerment. We can define resistance as the ability of an individual actor to attain an end or series of ends that serve to challenge and/or subvert domination. In order to accommodate the feminist interest in resistance, our conception of power must cover power-to as well.

Power-With

To satisfy the feminist interest in solidarity, our definition will also have to include a final sense of power. Feminists are interested in solidarity because we have an interest in understanding the kind of collective power that binds the feminist movement together and allies it with other social movements in such a way that we can formulate and achieve our goals. I take it that the goal of the feminist movement is not to put women in a position to exact at long last our revenge for the suffering we have endured under a heteropatriarchal society. Thus, it does not make sense to view the solidarity that enables the feminist movement to formulate and achieve its objectives as merely an instance of power-over.[19] Rather, the goal is a kind of collective empowerment. Moreover, because solidarity represents a *collective* empowerment, it is not completely described by power-to, as I have defined it. If solidarity cannot be viewed as a way of exercising either power-over or power-to, feminists require a third sense of power—namely, power-with.

Power-with is the sense that emerges out of Arendt's definition of power as "the human ability not just to act but to act in concert."[20] Understood in this way, power is a collective ability that results from the receptivity and reciprocity that characterize the relations among individual members of the collectivity.[21] Drawing on these aspects of Arendt's understanding of power, we can offer the following definition of power-with: the ability of a collectivity to act together for the attainment of an agreed-upon end or series of ends.

However, *solidarity* and *power-with* cannot be considered equivalent terms. For example, a military group that is unjustly exercising power over a population by imposing martial law can be said to be exercising power-with. In fact, this collective power-with may well be what allows the military to maintain its position of dominance. Yet this does not completely correspond to the kind of solidarity in which feminists are interested. Thus, just as we concluded that domination is a particular way of exercising power-over and resistance a particular way of exercising power-to, solidarity should be understood as a particular way of exercising power-with. With that in mind, I define solidarity as the ability of a collectivity to act together for the agreed-upon end of challenging, subverting, and, ultimately, overturning a system of domination.

Having started with what interests feminists when we are interested in power, we have arrived at three desiderata for a general definition of power: It will have to include power-over, power-to, and power-with. To satisfy these desiderata, our definition of power will have to be quite broad. Thus, I will define power simply as the ability or capacity of an actor or set of actors to act. This rather broad definition has two benefits. First, it easily includes all three of the senses of power that I have delineated. Power-over is the ability or capacity to act in such a way as to constrain the choices available to another actor or set of actors; power-to is the individual ability or capacity to act so as to attain some end; and power-with is the collective ability or capacity to act together so as to attain some common or shared end. Because it can include power-over, power-to, and power-with, our definition can accommodate feminists' interests in understanding domination, resistance, and solidarity. The second benefit of this definition is that it accords nicely with the etymology of the term: *Power* is derived from the Latin *potere* and the French *pouvoir*, both of which mean *to be able*.

Defining power in this way, however, does have its drawbacks, the most significant of which is that many social and political theorists define it differently. Many theorists equate power with only one of the three senses that I have delineated, usually power-over.[22] But although my definition does not capture all aspects of standard usage, it is better suited than others to the interests that feminists bring to the study of power. If we want to satisfy these interests, we have to define power in such a way.

Another potential objection to defining power in this way is that it seems to privilege one of the three senses of power that I have distinguished—namely, power-to. If power is defined as the ability or capacity to act, then it is barely distinguishable from power-to, which is defined as the individual ability or capacity to act so as to attain some end. This might seem to cause problems for my argument in Chapter 1. There, I argued that power cannot simply be equated with empowerment or power-to; yet my own definition might seem to understand power in precisely that way. Thus, it seems that I have sided with the empowerment theorists after all.

Yet I have not, in this broad definition, simply sided with the empowerment theorists. My argument in Chapter 1 against the power-as-domination and power-as-empowerment models was that each of these conceptions yields a one-sided view of power. It was never my contention that the empowerment theorists have a wholly incorrect understanding of power; I claimed only that their understanding is incomplete because they tend to view their conception of power *in opposition to* the view held by the domination theorists. The following passage from Held is instructive in this regard:

> The relation between mothering person and child . . . yields a *new view* of power. We are accustomed to thinking of power as something that can be wielded by one person over another, a means by which one person can bend another to his will. . . . But consider now *the very different view* of power in the relation between the mothering person and child. The superior power of the mothering person is useless for most of what she aims to achieve in bringing up the child. The mothering person seeks to empower the child to act responsibly; she neither wants to "wield" power nor to defend herself against the power "wielded" by the child.[23]

In this passage, Held presents the conception of power as empowerment as radically different from a conception that defines power as a form of power-over, or, more specifically, as domination.

I contend that it makes no sense to think of these two conceptions of power as opposed to one another. As Foucault and Butler argue quite persuasively, domination and empowerment are always intertwined with respect to the subject; one is always subject to relations of domination and yet simultaneously empowered to take up the position of a subject in and through that subjection. Moreover, these different modalities of power are not just interrelated in practice, they are conceptually interrelated. Exercising power-over always presupposes exercising power-to: In order to exercise power over another, one must exercise power in the sense of the capacity or ability to act in such a way as to attain some end. Similarly, exercising power-with presupposes exercising power-to: For a group to exercise power in the sense of the collective capacity to act so as to attain some agreed-upon end, the individual members of that group must also exercise power in the sense of the individual capacity to act so as to attain some end. Although power-to is the most basic of the three senses that I have delineated, it is not opposed to either power-over or power-with.

This conceptual interrelatedness brings out an important aspect of my account of power: In my view, power-over, power-to, and power-with are not best understood as distinct *types* or *forms* of power; rather, they represent analytically distinguishable *features* of a situation. Just as Arendt noted that, despite the careful analytical distinctions she draws among violence, power, authority, and strength, all of these phenomena may be present in the same situation, I acknowledge that although power-over, power-to, and power-with are analytically distinguishable features of a situation, they may all be present in one interaction. For instance, an action that is made possible by collective power-with necessarily presupposes the power-to of individual members of the collectivity and may also be used as a means to achieving power over others. The feminist struggle over the Equal Rights Amendment provides a nice illustration of this point. In their struggle to pass the ERA, a group of individual actors worked together to achieve the agreed-upon goal of passing a constitutional amendment that, had it passed, would have constrained the options of those who were in a position to or wanted to discriminate against women. The advantage of the definition of power that I have sketched out is that it provides a set of analytical tools that can help us make sense of the complex power relations at work in such a situation.

Methodological Considerations

I began this chapter by asking the question "What interests feminists when we are interested in power?" In the previous section, I offered a definition of the concept of power that was designed to address those interests. I argued that feminists need a conception of power that can illuminate power-over, power-to, and power-with, because only such a theory will be able to satisfy feminists' diverse interests in understanding domination, resistance, and solidarity.

The next step is to sketch out a methodological approach to the study of power that will enable us to theorize domination, resistance, and solidarity, and the ways in which they are interrelated. Elucidating the interplay between each of these ways of exercising power is crucial because only such an integrative approach will be complex enough to make sense of the multiple and overlapping power relations within which we women find ourselves. In the remainder of this chapter, I shall map out a series of analytic perspectives on power that are designed to help illuminate the multifarious relations of domination, resistance, and solidarity with which feminists are concerned.

The two primary analytic perspectives from which feminists ought to be able to view power relations are what I will call the *foreground perspective* and the *background perspective*. The foreground perspective targets particular power relations between individuals or groups of individuals. One might, for example, adopt this analytic perspective to examine the particular instance of domination that exists when a husband is physically abusive to his wife, or when the wife resists her husband's abuse, or when a feminist group on a college campus collectively protests domestic violence. The background perspective, on the other hand, focuses on the background social conditions that allow these particular power relations to appear. It examines the subject-positions, cultural meanings, practices, institutions, and structures that make up the context within which particular power relations are able to emerge. From this perspective, one would be able to understand how a particular case of wife battery is made possible by the background subject-positions of "wife" and "husband"; by cultural definitions of masculinity and femininity; by certain habitual social practices; by the institutions of marriage, the judiciary, and the police; and by structural patterns of advantage and disadvantage between men and women—all of which create and continually reinforce the subordination of women. Similarly, one would be able to see how a wife's resistance to such domination and a feminist group's collective protest are made possible by an alternative set of background subject-positions, cultural meanings, practices, and so on.

The Foreground Perspective

From the foreground perspective, the aim is to describe the power relation that exists between individuals or discrete groups of individuals. Thus, with respect to domination, from this perspective one could examine how, for example, a particular husband is able to dominate his wife through physical force, emotional manipulation, coercion, intimidation, and the like. Similarly, from this perspective, one could study the ways in which the wife is able to resist her abusive husband by, for instance, going to a shelter for battered women, pressing charges against him, or calling a divorce lawyer. Finally, one could study the solidarity that emerges out of collective protests against violence against women in such arenas as "Take Back the Night" marches and out of the collective action that leads to the founding of shelters for battered women.

However, an analysis that viewed power solely from the foreground perspective would be incomplete and inadequate for two reasons. First, a particular power relation, studied in isolation from its cultural, practical, institutional, and structural context, is easily perceived as an anomaly. Thus, for example, viewed solely from the foreground perspective, a particular case of wife battery may seem to be merely the product of a bad relationship or a violent temper, and not part of the larger system of the subordination of women. Second, there is a high degree of interplay between the relations highlighted by foreground and background perspectives. On the one hand, the particular power relations that are the focus of the foreground perspective always occur in the context of a set of background social relations that shape the expectations, choices, and beliefs of the individuals involved. On the other hand, these particular power relations themselves help to shape and mold the set of social relations that are the focus of the background perspective; indeed, in some sense, these social relations are just the accumulated or sedimented effects of a bunch of particular power relations. Thus, the foreground/background distinction is an analytical one; it is a distinction between different angles to take when one studies power relations in society. Accordingly, each perspective is necessary for a full illumination of the other.

The Background Perspective

The background perspective, which focuses on the complex social relations that ground every particular power relation, is considerably more complex than the foreground perspective. This perspective on power has similarities to Wartenberg's "situated conception of power." This conception, Wartenberg writes, "conceptualizes the role of 'peripheral social others.' By calling this account of power 'situated,' I stress the fact that the power dyad is itself situated in the context of other social relations through which it is actually constituted as a power relationship."[24] As Wartenberg points out, a specific power relation must be situated within a larger context in order to understand how it is "actually constituted as a power relationship." In other words, we need to view power from what I am calling the background perspective in order to understand how relations between distinct individuals come to be, so to speak, "power-ed."

The background perspective can be further differentiated into five distinct aspects: subject-positions, cultural meanings, social practices, institutions, and structures. I discuss each of these aspects in turn.

Subject-Positions. The aim of this analytic perspective is to highlight the constitutive role that power relations play in the formation of subject-positions that are available for individuals to occupy. In other words, when viewing power from this perspective, feminists might theorize the various subject-positions that are available to women. Further, this perspective allows feminists to understand the ways in which those subject-positions actually *position* women in a network of power relations.[25] Feminists need this analytic perspective to investigate the fact that women's positions within this network tend to perpetuate the domination of women and discourage women's resistance and feminist solidarity. However, we also need to be attentive to the fact that women are never locked into one subject-position; rather, as Chantal Mouffe argues, individuals constantly move from one position to another, depending on their context. As a result, as Mouffe puts it, "the 'identity' of such a multiple and contradictory subject is . . . always contingent and precarious, temporarily fixed at the intersection of those subject positions and dependent on specific forms of identification."[26] Understanding the multiple and sometimes contradictory nature of subject-positions is crucial for feminist theorizing of the complex ways in which particular women can be positioned differently within the context of one and the same norm, practice, or institution.

Cultural Meanings.   A feminist conception of power must also be able to examine power relations in terms of culturally encoded meanings and definitions. For example, a feminist analysis of power operating from this perspective must examine the way that key concepts such as femininity, masculinity, and sexuality are defined in a given cultural context. Similarly, it must pay attention to the ways in which the feminist movement contests culturally hegemonic definitions and proposes alternate, subversive definitions that can then become resources for individual women who are attempting to resist male domination. Finally, in the course of these examinations, such an analysis must be attentive to the way the meanings ascribed to "femininity," "masculinity," "sexuality," and the like vary widely with race, ethnicity, class, and sexual orientation.

For instance, according to certain culturally hegemonic definitions, to be "feminine" is to be passive, cooperative, and obedient, whereas to be "masculine" is to be aggressive, competitive, and in control. An examination of these definitions of masculinity and femininity has helped feminists to understand one of the factors that explains, for example, how particular husbands are able to assume positions of domination over their wives. However, some women who are dominated through marriage make use of the feminist critique of patriarchal definitions of "femininity" and "masculinity" as resources with which to resist such domination.[27] Moreover, as black feminists have pointed out, although the equation of "femininity" with passivity applies well to a discussion of middle-class white women, it does not apply well to a discussion of black women. Thus, in order to do justice to the complexity of power relations viewed from the perspective of cultural meanings, feminists must interrogate the different definitions of femininity, masculinity, sexuality, and the like that are applied to different women.

Social Practices. These multiple, culturally encoded understandings of femininity, masculinity, and sexuality are reflected in the third aspect of the background perspective—namely, the development of particular social practices. Thus, a feminist analysis that examines power from the background perspective needs to study the ways in which such understandings are intertwined with relevant practices. For example, a common (although far from universal) ideal practice in traditional gender-structured marriages between middle-class whites has been for wives to stay home and assume primary responsibility for housework and child care while husbands participate in the world of waged work. Indeed, this practice cannot be understood in isolation from the understandings of "true" (white, middle-class) femininity and masculinity that it upholds. Moreover, as feminists have pointed out, this practice reinforces male domination of women on a number of levels: For example, it renders individual wives more subject to domination from their husbands because lacking personal income and the skills that make them employable outside the home leaves wives with fewer "exit options," which in turn will make them more likely to put up with abuse.[28] However, individual wives and husbands can also draw on the resources provided by the feminist movement and attempt to build their marriages around practices that enable wives to resist male domination: For example, if both wife and husband work for wages and share the responsibility for work inside the home equally, then wives will be more likely to have exit options that put them in a better position successfully to resist domination when it occurs.[29]

It is important to note here that cultural meanings are often internalized and social practices often become habitual—phenomena to which a feminist analysis must pay careful attention, since they make feminist attempts to subvert and overthrow the subordination of women more difficult. By consciously or unconsciously internalizing hegemonic cultural meanings and by performing certain social practices by force of habit, a dominated individual can come to accept meanings and adopt practices that reflect and reinforce the power of those who dominate. For example, if a married woman has internalized the notion that to be feminine is to be passive, she may be less likely actively to assert her need for an equal share of the couple's resources, and the resulting lack of equity in the distribution of resources will reinforce the wife's subordinate position. The practice of habitually deferring to the husband's judgment with respect to financial matters will have a similar effect. If such practices become habitual and such definitions are internalized, the task of introducing new practices and meanings that offer women resources that help them resist subordination is rendered that much more difficult.

Institutions.   Feminists should also be prepared to study power from the perspective of the institutional contexts in which subject-positions, cultural meanings, and social practices are embedded. Institutions may reinforce and uphold power relations by endorsing specific understandings of femininity or masculinity, or by encouraging or forbidding particular practices. For example, all corporations operate with particular understandings of masculinity and femininity that are influential in corporate hiring and promotion policies. In the crassest instances, these policies are explicitly different for those who are on the so-called mommy track than for those who are not. More broadly, few corporations have on-site childcare, as the work world is normally structured on the assumption that the worker will either be childless or have a wife. Such understandings of masculine and feminine roles also play a crucial role in judicial decisions in divorce cases regarding custody of children and division of marital assets. Moreover, these institutions often establish social practices that reinforce the domination of women. For example, the fact that corporations still pay women less than men for comparable work and channel women into the low-pay, low-status jobs that make up the pink-collar ghetto reinforces the larger practice in which some women stay at home while their husbands work for pay. On the other hand, institutions that have been created and sustained by the feminist movement can provide resources for women who seek to resist male domination. For example, the network of battered women's shelters offers institutional support as well as conceptual and normative resources for abused and battered wives to resist that exercise of domination.

Structures.   Finally, viewing power from the background perspective involves understanding the structural aspects of power relations. There are two senses in which power can be analyzed from a structural perspective. The first sense understands structures as observed, *de facto* patterns of power distribution. In this sense, a structural analysis of power involves, for example, what Nancy Fraser and Linda Nicholson have characterized as the "identification and critique of macrostructures of inequality and injustice which cut across the boundaries separating relatively discrete practices and institutions."[30] According to Fraser and Nicholson, such an analysis allows "for critique of pervasive axes of stratification, for critique of broad-based relations of dominance and subordination along lines like gender, race, and class."[31] Viewing power from this analytic perspective enables us to make such general claims as "people of color are dominated by whites," "women are dominated by men," "women of color are dominated by white women," and so on. Further, it allows us to assert that these statements can have meaning across stretches of time and within many diverse cultures, even though the particular forms that domination takes in various times and cultures will usually be quite different. From this perspective, feminists must also examine the possibilities for individual and collective resistance that are both created and excluded by any given structure of power relations. As this kind of structural perspective on power is concerned with the emergence of observed patterns of power distribution, it analyzes power in terms of what I will call *surface structures*. However, we must exercise caution here. As Foucault warned, we must be careful not to find domination wherever we happen to go looking for it. Thus, when we analyze power from the perspective of surface structures we should be careful not to impose, in a top-down fashion, a rubric for understanding all social relations; instead, we should be attentive to the ways that this *de facto* structure of power relations emerges out of a consideration of particular power relations.

This perspective on the structural nature of power can be contrasted with one that views power in terms of what I will call *deep structures*. In this second sense, to analyze power from a structural perspective is to appeal to an explanatory framework that can illuminate or explicate the observed patterns of power relations that emerge as surface structures. Feminists have examined power relations within marriages, for example, in terms of deep power structures such as the gender division of labor. Women who work in the home are not paid, and women who work for wages tend to work in low-pay, low-skill, and low-status occupations. This pattern in turn *structures* the possibilities for the kinds of dyadic power relations individuals can have, the kinds of subject-positions available for them to occupy, the cultural meanings they are likely to employ, the social practices they are likely to adopt, and the institutions to which they can easily have access. Thus, one might say that viewing power from the perspective of deep structures involves examining the ways in which power relations actually structure our social situation, whereas from the surface perspective, power relations are viewed as a structure.[32]

* * *

In this final chapter, I have sought to accomplish two tasks: first, drawing on the insights gained by our analyses of Foucault, Butler, and Arendt in earlier chapters, to define power and some key power terms according to the kinds of interests that feminists bring to the study of power; and, second, to sketch out a methodology for analyzing power consisting of a series of perspectives from which power so defined might best be analyzed. Taken together, this definition of power and these methodological considerations provide a feminist conception of power that can illuminate the complex and multifarious relations of domination, resistance, and solidarity with which feminism is concerned.

Notes

1. I borrow this phrase from Robert Dahl (see Dahl, "Power as the Control of Behavior," in Steven Lukes, ed., *Power* [New York: New York University Press, 1986], p. 40). Dahl's list of power terms is much more extensive than the list I will develop here.

2. Steven Lukes, "Introduction," in Lukes, ed., *Power*, pp. 4–5. For a similar claim, see William Connolly, *The Terms of Political Discourse* (Princeton: Princeton University Press, 1983), p. 126.

3. The conception of power presented here may turn out to be useful for comprehending and contesting racism and heterosexism as well. I call this a "feminist" theory of power more for its theoretical focus than for its methodology. However, because investigating women's subordination necessarily involves investigating relations of dominance and subordination based on race, class, ethnicity, sexual orientation, and so on, the possible applicability of this approach to the study of power on other axes of stratification seems to me to be one of its greatest strengths.

4. For an extended account of this problem, see Elizabeth Spelman, *Inessential Woman: Problems of Exclusion in Feminist Thought* (Boston: Beacon, 1989).

5. Thomas Wartenberg, *The Forms of Power: From Domination to Transformation* (Philadelphia: Temple University Press, 1990), p. 85.

6. Wartenberg explicitly argues that power must be defined with reference to intentional concepts (see ibid., pp. 62–65.)

7. Lukes, "Introduction," p. 1.

8. Wartenberg recognizes this aspect of male domination, but he does not seem to recognize that his definition of power-over as strategic is in tension with this recognition. (See Wartenberg, *Forms of Power*, pp. 155–157.)

9. For an account of decisions and nondecisions with respect to the study of power, see Peter Bachrach and Morton Baratz, "Two Faces of Power," in Roderick Bell et al., eds., *Political Power: A Reader in Theory and Research* (New York: Free Press, 1969), and "Decisions and Non-decisions: An Analytic Framework," *American Political Science Review* 57 (1963): 632–644.

10. On the importance of anticipated reactions in the study of power, see Jack Nagel, *The Descriptive Analysis of Power* (New Haven: Yale University Press, 1975).

11. On the importance of accounting for more than merely avowed interests in the definition of power, see Steven Lukes, *Power: A Radical View* (London: Macmillan, 1974).

12. For a critique of dyadic and interventional models of power-over, see Wartenberg, *Forms of Power*, pp. 65–69; and Nancy Fraser, "Beyond the Master/Subject Model: Reflections on Carole Pateman's *Sexual Contract*," *Social Text* 37 (1993): 173–181.

13. Coaching would thus be an instance of what Wartenberg calls "transformative power." (See Wartenberg, *Forms of Power*, especially chs. 9 and 10.) The instances of transformative power that he discusses are teaching, parenting, and therapy.

14. On this point, see Wartenberg: "A relation between two agents is an instance of domination only if the dominated agent is specifically harmed through the relationship" (Wartenberg, *Forms of Power*, p. 118).

15. Here I part company with Wartenberg, who argues that theorists of power should focus their attention on power-over. (See Wartenberg, *Forms of Power*, passim.)

16. See, for example, Virginia Held, *Feminist Morality: Transforming Culture, Society, and Politics* (Chicago: University of Chicago Press, 1993), pp. 136–137.

17. Here I am following William Connolly's characterization of power-to. (See Connolly, *Terms of Political Discourse*, pp. 86–87.)

18. This raises the issue of the conceptual interdependence of *power-over* and *power-to*. I shall address that issue in a moment.

19. I say *merely* here because achieving a kind of power-over those who are in a position of dominance and would like to remain there may be a particular feminist goal. In other words, in some cases, feminists may have to use power over others to achieve the kind of changes that we strive to achieve. On this point, see Jane Mansbridge, "Using Power/Fighting Power," *Constellations* 1 (1994): 53–73.

20. Hannah Arendt, *On Violence* (New York: Harcourt, Brace, and Co., 1969), p. 44.

21. For a discussion of these aspects of power-with, see Mary Parker Follett, "Power," in Henry C. Metcalf and L. Urwick, eds., *Dynamic Administration: The Collected Papers of Mary Parker Follett* (New York: Harper and Brothers, 1942), pp. 95–116.

22. However, there is a tradition in political theory that defines power more broadly than this. The most notable historical example is Hobbes's definition of power as the "present means to obtain some future apparent good." I am grateful to my colleague Bernard Gert for reminding me of Hobbes's interesting discussion of power. (See Thomas Hobbes, *Leviathan*, ed. Edwin Curley [Indianapolis: Hackett Publishing Co., 1994], p. 50.) Twentieth-century exceptions to this trend include C. B. Macpherson, who argues that political theorists need to investigate both power-over and power-to, and Jane Mansbridge, whose definition of power as "the actual or potential causal relation between the interests of an actor or set of actors and the outcome itself" includes both power-over and power-to. (See Macpherson, *Democratic Theory: Essays in Retrieval* [Oxford: Oxford University Press, 1973]; and Mansbridge, "Using Power/Fighting Power," pp. 55–56.)

23. Held, *Feminist Morality*, p. 209; emphasis added.

24. Wartenberg, *Forms of Power*, p. 142. The major difference between my account and Wartenberg's is that his is solely concerned with power-over, whereas mine attempts to cover power-to and power-with as well. On this point, see Wartenberg, *Forms of Power*, pp. 27ff.

25. On this point, see the discussion of "positionality" in Linda Alcoff, "Cultural Feminism Versus Post-Structuralism: The Identity Crisis in Feminist Theory," *Signs* 13 (1988): 428ff.

26. Chantal Mouffe, "Democratic Politics and the Question of Identity," in John Rajchman, ed., *The Identity in Question* (New York: Routledge, 1995), p. 33.

27. For a discussion of how women who are not feminist activists or scholars use such resources in their daily lives, see Jane Mansbridge, "The Role of Dis-

course in the Feminist Movement," paper delivered at the annual meeting of the American Political Science Association, September 2–5, 1993.

28. For a discussion of the effects of traditional marriage on women's power, see Susan Moller Okin, *Justice, Gender, and the Family* (New York: Basic Books, 1989), ch. 7.

29. Of course, shared wage and house work will address only one of the many ways in which women's subordination is perpetuated through marriage. Even if both partners work for wages, the wife's wages will probably be significantly lower than the husband's, thus affecting the power relations in the relationship.

30. Nancy Fraser and Linda J. Nicholson, "Social Criticism Without Philosophy: An Encounter Between Feminism and Postmodernism," in Linda J. Nicholson, ed., *Feminism/ Postmodernism* (New York: Routledge, 1990), p. 23.

31. Ibid.

32. For a discussion of power as both structuring and structured, see Pierre Bourdieu, *Outline of a Theory of Practice*, trans. Richard Nice (Cambridge, Eng.: Cambridge University Press, 1977).

Bibliography

Alcoff, Linda. "Cultural Feminism Versus Poststructuralism: The Identity Crisis in Feminist Theory." *Signs: Journal of Women in Culture and Society* 13:3 (1988): 405–436.

_____. "Feminist Politics and Foucault: The Limits to a Collaboration." In *Crises in Continental Philosophy,* edited by Arlene Dallery and Charles Scott. Albany: SUNY Press, 1990.

Allen, Amy. "The Anti-Subjective Hypothesis: Michel Foucault and the Eradication of the Subject." Paper presented at the annual meeting of the American Philosophical Association, Eastern Division, Philadelphia, December 1997.

_____. "Foucault's Debt to Hegel." *Philosophy Today* 42:1 (1998): 71–78.

Arendt, Hannah. *Between Past and Future.* New York: Penguin, 1968.

_____. *Eichmann in Jerusalem: A Report on the Banality of Evil.* New York: Penguin, 1963.

_____. *The Human Condition.* Chicago: University of Chicago Press, 1958.

_____. *Lectures on Kant's Political Philosophy.* Chicago: University of Chicago Press, 1982.

_____. *Men in Dark Times.* New York: Harcourt, Brace, and World, 1968.

_____. *On Revolution.* New York: Penguin, 1963.

_____. *On Violence.* New York: Harcourt, Brace, and Co., 1969.

_____. *The Origins of Totalitarianism.* New edition (3 vols. in 1). New York: Harcourt, Brace, and Co., 1973.

_____. "Reflections on Little Rock." *Dissent* 6 (1959): 45–56.

Bachrach, Peter, and Morton Baratz. "Decisions and Non-decisions: An Analytic Framework." *American Political Science Review* 57 (1963): 632–644.

_____. "Two Faces of Power." In *Political Power: A Reader in Theory and Research,* edited by Roderick Bell et al. New York: Free Press, 1969.

Bar On, Bat-Ami. "Marginality and Epistemic Privilege." In *Feminist Epistemologies,* edited by Linda Alcoff and Elizabeth Potter. New York: Routledge, 1993.

Bartky, Sandra. "Foucault, Femininity, and the Modernization of Patriarchal Power." In Bartky, *Femininity and Domination.* New York: Routledge, 1990.

Benhabib, Seyla. *The Reluctant Modernism of Hannah Arendt.* London: Sage, 1996.

_____. *Situating the Self: Gender, Community, and Postmodernism in Contemporary Ethics.* New York: Routledge, 1992.

Benhabib, Seyla, Judith Butler, Drucilla Cornell, and Nancy Fraser. *Feminist Contentions: A Philosophical Exchange,* edited by Linda J. Nicholson. New York: Routledge, 1995.

Bohman, James. "The Moral Costs of Political Pluralism: The Dilemmas of Difference and Equality in Arendt's 'Reflections on Little Rock.'" In *Hannah Arendt:*

Twenty Years Later, edited by Larry May and Jerome Kohn. Cambridge, Mass.: MIT Press, 1996.

Bordo, Susan. "Anorexia Nervosa: Psychopathology as the Crystallization of Culture." In Bordo, *Unbearable Weight: Feminism, Western Culture, and the Body*. Berkeley: University of California Press, 1993.

_____. "Postmodern Subjects, Postmodern Bodies, Postmodern Resistance." In Bordo, *Unbearable Weight: Feminism, Western Culture, and the Body*. Berkeley: University of California Press, 1993.

Bourdieu, Pierre. "La Domination Masculine." *Actes de la recherche en sciences sociales* 84 (1990): 2–31.

_____. *Outline of a Theory of Practice*, translated by Richard Nice. Cambridge, Eng.: Cambridge University Press, 1977.

Brown, Wendy. *Manhood and Politics*. Totowa, N.J.: Rowman and Littlefield, 1988.

Butler, Judith. *Bodies That Matter: On the Discursive Limits of "Sex."* New York: Routledge, 1993.

_____. *Excitable Speech: Toward a Politics of the Performative*. New York: Routledge, 1997.

_____. *Gender Trouble: Feminism and the Subversion of Identity*. New York: Routledge, 1990.

_____. *The Psychic Life of Power: Theories in Subjection*. Stanford: Stanford University Press, 1997.

_____. "Sexual Inversions." In *Discourses of Sexuality: From Aristotle to AIDS*, edited by Donna Stanton. Ann Arbor: University of Michigan Press, 1992.

_____. *Subjects of Desire: Hegelian Reflections in Twentieth-Century France*. New York: Columbia University Press, 1987.

Canovan, Margaret. *Hannah Arendt: A Reinterpretation of Her Political Thought*. Cambridge, Eng.: Cambridge University Press, 1992.

Cixous, Hélène. "Entrieten avec Françoise van Rossum-Guyon." *Revue des sciences humaines* 168 (1977): 479–493.

Connolly, William. *The Terms of Political Discourse*. Princeton: Princeton University Press, 1983.

Cutting-Gray, Joanne. "Hannah Arendt, Feminism, and the Politics of Alterity: 'What Will We Lose If We Win?'" *Hypatia* 8:1 (Winter 1993): 35–54.

Dahl, Robert. "Power as the Control of Behavior." In *Power*, edited by Steven Lukes. New York: New York University Press, 1986.

Dean, Jodi. *Solidarity of Strangers: Feminism After Identity Politics*. Berkeley: University of California Press, 1996.

Derrida, Jacques. "Signature, Event, Context." In *Limited, Inc.*, edited by Gerald Graff, translated by Samuel Weber and Jeffrey Mehlman. Evanston: Northwestern University Press, 1988.

Diamond, Irene, and Lee Quinby, eds. *Feminism and Foucault: Reflections on Resistance*. Boston: Northeastern University Press, 1988.

Dietz, Mary. "Feminist Receptions of Hannah Arendt." In *Feminist Interpretations of Hannah Arendt*, edited by Bonnie Honig. University Park: Pennsylvania State Press, 1995.

_____. "Hannah Arendt and Feminist Politics." In *Hannah Arendt: Critical Essays*, edited by Lewis P. Hinchman and Sandra K. Hinchman. Albany: SUNY Press, 1994.

Disch, Lisa Jane. *Hannah Arendt and the Limits of Philosophy*. Ithaca: Cornell University Press, 1994.

_____. "On Friendship in 'Dark Times.'" In *Rereading the Canon: Feminist Interpretations of Hannah Arendt*, edited by Bonnie Honig. University Park: Pennsylvania State Press, 1995.

Dworkin, Andrea. *Intercourse*. New York: Free Press, 1987.

_____. *Pornography: Men Possessing Women*. New York: Plume, 1979.

Elshtain, Jean Bethke. *Meditations on Modern Political Thought: Masculine/Feminine Themes from Luther to Arendt*. New York: Praeger, 1986.

Flax, Jane. *Thinking Fragments: Psychoanalysis, Feminism, and Postmodernism in the Contemporary West*. Berkeley: University of California Press, 1990.

Follett, Mary Parker. "Power." In *Dynamic Administration: The Collected Papers of Mary Parker Follett*, edited by Henry C. Metcalf and L. Urwick. New York: Harper and Brothers, 1942.

Foucault, Michel. "Afterword: The Subject and Power." In Hubert Dreyfus and Paul Rabinow, *Michel Foucault: Beyond Structuralism and Hermeneutics*, 2nd ed. Chicago: University of Chicago Press, 1982.

_____. *The Archaeology of Knowledge and the Discourse on Language*, translated by A. M. Sheridan Smith. New York: Pantheon, 1972.

_____. *The Care of the Self: Volume Three of the History of Sexuality*, translated by Robert Hurley. New York: Vintage, 1986.

_____. *Discipline and Punish: The Birth of the Prison*, translated by Alan Sheridan. New York: Vintage, 1979.

_____. "The Ethic of Care for the Self as a Practice of Freedom." In *The Final Foucault*, edited by James Bernauer and David Rasmussen. Cambridge, Mass.: MIT Press, 1988.

_____. *The Foucault Reader*, edited by Paul Rabinow. New York: Pantheon, 1984.

_____. *The History of Sexuality, Volume One: An Introduction*, translated by Robert Hurley. New York: Vintage, 1978.

_____. *Language, Counter-Memory, Practice*, edited by Donald F. Bouchard. Ithaca: Cornell University Press, 1977.

_____. *Michel Foucault: Politics, Philosophy, Culture*, edited by Lawrence D. Kritzman. New York: Routledge, 1988.

_____. *The Order of Things: An Archaeology of the Human Sciences*. New York: Vintage, 1973.

_____. *Power/Knowledge: Selected Interviews and Other Writings 1972–1977*, edited by Colin Gordon. New York: Pantheon, 1980.

_____. *The Use of Pleasure: Volume Two of the History of Sexuality*, translated by Robert Hurley. New York: Vintage, 1985.

Fraser, Nancy. "Beyond the Master/Subject Model: Reflections on Carole Pateman's *Sexual Contract*." *Social Text* 37 (1993): 173–181.

_____. "False Antitheses: A Response to Seyla Benhabib and Judith Butler." *Praxis International* 11:2 (1991): 166–177.

_____. "Foucault on Modern Power: Empirical Insights and Normative Confusions." In Fraser, *Unruly Practices: Power, Gender, and Discourse in Contemporary Critical Theory*. Minneapolis: University of Minnesota Press, 1989.

_____. "Michel Foucault: A 'Young Conservative'?" In Fraser, *Unruly Practices: Power, Gender, and Discourse in Contemporary Critical Theory*. Minneapolis: University of Minnesota Press, 1989.

_____. "Rethinking the Public Sphere: A Contribution to the Critique of an Actually Existing Democracy." *Social Text* 25/26 (1990): 56–80.

_____. "Struggle over Needs: Outline of a Socialist-Feminist Critical Theory of Late Capitalist Political Culture." In Fraser, *Unruly Practices: Power, Gender, and Discourse in Contemporary Critical Theory*. Minneapolis: University of Minnesota Press, 1989.

_____. "Women, Welfare, and the Politics of Need Interpretation" In Fraser, *Unruly Practices: Power, Gender, and Discourse in Contemporary Critical Theory*. Minneapolis: University of Minnesota Press, 1989.

Fraser, Nancy, and Linda Gordon. "A Genealogy of 'Dependency': Tracing a Keyword of the U.S. Welfare State." *Signs* 19:2 (1994): 309–336.

Fraser, Nancy, and Linda J. Nicholson. "Social Criticism Without Philosophy: An Encounter Between Feminism and Postmodernism." In *Feminism/Postmodernism*, edited by Linda J. Nicholson. New York: Routledge, 1990.

Fultner, Barbara. "Habermas and Butler on Universality and Idealisation." Paper presented at the Fifth Annual Critical Theory Roundtable, St. Louis University, September 26–28, 1997.

Gilligan, Carol. *In a Different Voice: Psychological Theory and Women's Development*. Cambridge, Mass.: Harvard University Press, 1982.

Habermas, Jürgen. "Hannah Arendt's Communications Concept of Power." In *Hannah Arendt: Critical Essays*, edited by Lewis P. Hinchman and Sandra K. Hinchman. Albany: SUNY Press, 1994.

_____. "Modernity Versus Post-Modernity." *New German Critique* 22 (1981): 3–14.

_____. *The Philosophical Discourse of Modernity*, translated by Frederick G. Lawrence. Cambridge, Mass.: MIT Press, 1987.

Harris, Angela P. "Race and Essentialism in Feminist Legal Theory." In *Feminist Legal Theory: Readings in Law and Gender*, edited by Katharine T. Bartlett and Rosanne Kennedy. Boulder: Westview Press, 1991.

Hartsock, Nancy. "Community/Sexuality/Gender: Rethinking Power." In *Revisioning the Political: Feminist Reconstructions of Traditional Concepts in Western Political Theory*, edited by Nancy J. Hirschmann and Christine Di Stefano. Boulder: Westview Press, 1996.

_____. "Foucault on Power: A Theory for Women?" In *Feminism/Postmodernism*, edited by Linda J. Nicholson. New York: Routledge, 1990.

_____. *Money, Sex, and Power: Toward a Feminist Historical Materialism*. Boston: Northeastern University Press, 1983.

Havel, Vaclav. "The Power of the Powerless." In Havel et al., *The Power of the Powerless: Citizens Against the State in Central-Eastern Europe*. New York: ME Sharpe, Inc., 1985.

Hegel, G.W.F. *Vorlesungen über die Geschichte der Philosophie*, edited by Johannes Hoffmeister. Leipzig: F. Meiner, 1938.

Hekman, Susan, ed. *Rereading the Canon: Feminist Interpretations of Foucault*. University Park: Pennsylvania State Press, 1996.

Held, Virginia. *Feminist Morality: Transforming Culture, Society, and Politics.* Chicago: University of Chicago Press, 1993.

Hoagland, Sarah Lucia. *Lesbian Ethics: Toward New Value.* Palo Alto, Calif.: Institute of Lesbian Studies, 1988.

Hobbes, Thomas. *Leviathan*, edited by Edwin Curley. Indianapolis: Hackett Publishing Co., 1994.

Honig, Bonnie. "Toward an Agonistic Feminism: Hannah Arendt and the Politics of Identity." In *Feminists Theorize the Political*, edited by Judith Butler and Joan W. Scott. New York: Routledge, 1992.

Honig, Bonnie, ed. *Rereading the Canon: Feminist Interpretations of Hannah Arendt.* University Park: Pennsylvania State Press, 1995.

Honneth, Axel. *The Critique of Power: Reflective Stages in a Critical Social Theory*, translated by Kenneth Baynes. Cambridge, Mass.: MIT Press, 1991.

Hoy, David Couzens, ed. *Foucault: A Critical Reader.* Oxford: Blackwell, 1986.

Irigaray, Luce. "And the One Doesn't Stir Without the Other," translated by Hélène Vivienne Wenzel. *Signs* 7:1 (1981): 60–67.

_____. *This Sex Which Is Not One*, translated by Catharine Porter. Ithaca: Cornell University Press, 1985.

Jay, Martin. "Hannah Arendt: Opposing Views." *Partisan Review* 45:3 (1978): 348–368.

Kaplan, Morris B. "Refiguring the Jewish Question: Arendt, Proust, and the Politics of Sexuality." In *Rereading the Canon: Feminist Interpretations of Hannah Arendt*, edited by Bonnie Honig. University Park: Pennsylvania State Press, 1995.

_____. *Sexual Justice: Democratic Citizenship and the Politics of Desire.* New York: Routledge, 1997.

Kateb, George. *Hannah Arendt: Politics, Conscience, Evil.* Totowa, N.J.: Rowman and Allanheld, 1983.

Kuykendall, Eléanor H. "Toward an Ethic of Nurturance: Irigaray on Mothering and Power." In *Mothering: Essays in Feminist Theory*, edited by Joyce Trebilcot. Savage, Md.: Rowman and Littlefield, 1983.

Lukes, Steven. *Power: A Radical View.* London: Macmillan, 1974.

Lukes, Steven, ed. *Power.* New York: New York University Press, 1986.

MacKinnon, Catharine. *Feminism Unmodified.* Cambridge, Mass.: Harvard University Press, 1987.

_____. *Only Words.* Cambridge, Mass.: Harvard University Press, 1993.

_____. *Toward a Feminist Theory of the State.* Cambridge, Mass.: Harvard University Press, 1989.

Macpherson, C. B. *Democratic Theory: Essays in Retrieval.* Oxford: Oxford University Press, 1973.

Mansbridge, Jane. "Feminism and Democratic Community." In *NOMOS XXXV: Democratic Community*, edited by John W. Chapman and Ian Shapiro. New York: New York University Press, 1993.

_____. "The Role of Discourse in the Feminist Movement." Paper presented at the annual American Political Science Association Meeting, Washington, D.C., September 1993.

_____. "Using Power/Fighting Power." *Constellations* 1 (1994): 53–73.

_____. *Why We Lost the ERA*. Chicago: University of Chicago Press, 1986.

May, Larry, and Jerome Kohn, eds. *Hannah Arendt: Twenty Years Later*. Cambridge, Mass.: MIT Press, 1996.

McCarthy, Thomas. "The Critique of Impure Reason: Foucault and the Frankfurt School." In McCarthy, *Ideals and Illusions: On Reconstruction and Deconstruction in Contemporary Critical Theory*. Cambridge, Mass.: MIT Press, 1991.

McNay, Lois. *Foucault and Feminism: Power, Gender, and the Self*. Boston: Northeastern University Press, 1992.

Mill, John Stuart. *The Subjection of Women*. Mineola, N.Y.: Dover, 1997.

Miller, Jean Baker. *Toward a New Psychology of Women*, 2nd ed. Boston: Beacon, 1986.

_____. "Women and Power." In *Rethinking Power*, edited by Thomas Wartenberg. Albany, NY: SUNY Press, 1992.

Mouffe, Chantal. "Democratic Politics and the Question of Identity." In *The Identity in Question*, edited by John Rajchman. New York: Routledge, 1995.

Nagel, Jack. *The Descriptive Analysis of Power*. New Haven: Yale University Press, 1975.

O'Brien, Mary. *The Politics of Reproduction*. Boston: Routledge and Kegan Paul, 1981.

Okin, Susan Moller. *Justice, Gender, and the Family*. New York: Basic Books, 1989.

_____. *Women in Western Political Thought*. Princeton: Princeton University Press, 1979.

Passerin d'Entreves, Alexander. *The Notion of the State: An Introduction to Political Theory*. Oxford: Oxford University Press, 1967.

Passerin d'Entreves, Maurizio. *The Political Philosophy of Hannah Arendt*. New York: Routledge, 1994.

Pateman, Carole. *The Sexual Contract*. Stanford: Stanford University Press, 1988.

Pitkin, Hanna Fenichel. "Justice: On Relating Private and Public." *Political Theory* 9:3 (1981): 327–352.

Rajchman, John, ed. *The Identity in Question*. New York: Routledge, 1995.

Rich, Adrienne. *Of Woman Born: Motherhood as Experience and Institution*. Tenth Anniversary Edition. New York: Norton, 1986.

_____. *On Lies, Secrets, and Silence: Selected Prose 1966–1978*. New York: W. W. Norton and Co., 1979.

Roiphe, Katie. *The Morning After: Sex, Fear, and Feminism on Campus*. New York: Little, Brown, 1993.

Ruddick, Sara. *Maternal Thinking: Toward a Politics of Peace*. New York: Ballantine, 1989.

_____. "Remarks on the Sexual Politics of Reason." In *Women and Moral Theory*, edited by Eva Feder Kittay and Diana T. Meyers. Lanham, Md.: Rowman and Littlefield, 1987.

Said, Edward. "Foucault and the Imagination of Power." In *Foucault: A Critical Reader*, edited by David Couzens Hoy. Oxford: Blackwell, 1986.

Sawicki, Jana. *Disciplining Foucault: Feminism, Power, and the Body*. New York: Routledge, 1991.

Scott, Joan Wallach. *Gender and the Politics of History*. New York: Columbia University Press, 1988.

Snitow, Ann, Christine Stansell, and Sharon Thompson, eds. *Powers of Desire: The Politics of Sexuality*. New York: Monthly Review Press, 1983.

Spelman, Elizabeth. *Inessential Woman: Problems of Exclusion in Feminist Thought*. Boston: Beacon, 1989.

Starhawk. *Truth or Dare: Encounters with Power, Authority, and Mystery*. San Francisco: Harper, 1987.

Vance, Carole S., ed. *Pleasure and Danger: Exploring Female Sexuality*. New York: Routledge, 1990.

Villa, Dana. *Arendt and Heidegger: The Fate of the Political*. Princeton: Princeton University Press, 1996.

Walzer, Michael. "The Politics of Michel Foucault." In *Foucault: A Critical Reader*, edited by David Couzens Hoy. Oxford: Blackwell, 1986.

Wartenberg, Thomas. *The Forms of Power: From Domination to Transformation*. Philadelphia: Temple University Press, 1990.

Weber, Max. *Economy and Society*, 3 vols. New York: Bedminster, 1968.

Weir, Allison. *Sacrificial Logics: Feminist Theory and the Critique of Identity*. New York: Routledge, 1996.

Wolf, Naomi. *Fire with Fire: The New Female Power and How It Will Change the 21st Century*. New York: Random House, 1993.

Yeatman, Anna. "Feminism and Power." In *Reconstructing Political Theory: Feminist Perspectives*, edited by Mary Shanley and Uma Narayan. University Park: Pennsylvania State University Press, 1997.

Young, Iris Marion. *Justice and the Politics of Difference*. Princeton: Princeton University Press, 1990.

Young-Bruehl, Elizabeth. *Hannah Arendt: For Love of the World*. New Haven: Yale University Press, 1982.

Zita, Jacqueline. Review of *Bodies That Matter*. *Signs* 21:3 (1996): 786–795.

Index